Skyhorse Publishing books may be purchased in bulk at special discounts for sales promotion, corporate gifts, fund-raising, or educational purposes. Special editions can also be created to specifications. For details, contact the Special Sales Department, Skyhorse Publishing, 307 West 36th Street, 11th Floor, New York, NY 10018 or info@skyhorsepublishing.com.

Skyhorse® and Skyhorse Publishing® are registered trademarks of Skyhorse Publishing, Inc.®, a Delaware corporation.

Visit our website at www.skyhorsepublishing.com.

10 9 8 7 6 5 4 3 2 1

Library of Congress Cataloging-in-Publication Data is available on file. Control Number: 2019045180

Cover design by Daniel Brount
Cover photo credit: Getty Images

Print ISBN: 978-1-5107-5464-5
Ebook ISBN: 978-1-5107-5372-3

Printed in China

Table of Contents

PART ONE: BACKGROUND

Introduction   2

Was This the Beginning of the Deep State?   6

The Myth and Deception of American Democracy   17

So You Heard about All This on TV and in
     the Newspapers, Huh?   22

From "Government of the People, by the People, for the People,"
     To "Government of Big Business, by Big Business, for Big
     Business"   30

How Collusion Occurs   38

American Money Powers Honed Its Skills from Historical Lessons
     Learned during Britain's Nineteenth Century Empire   44

PART TWO: THE TIMELINE

1832: The Demise of the Second Bank of the United States   50

Manifest Destiny: Domestic Imperialism   55

April 12, 1861: The Confederate Attack on Fort Sumter,
     Effectively Beginning the Worst Conflict in
     American History   62

1865: The Attempted Coup d'état of the United States
     of America   67

1881: The Assassination of President James Garfield—
     The First Successful Coup d'état in American History   85

1898: The Spanish-American War—Manifest Destiny Leaves
     the Continental US for the First Time   87

December 23, 1913: The Federal Reserve Act Is Signed
     into Law   95

1900–1917: The Military Goes to Work Protecting
    America's Sphere of Influence   103

1918: The Treaty of Versailles Ending World War I
    Was a Plan for a Second World War   106

The Great Depression   111

The Day of Infamy—or Was It the Day of Foreknowledge?   113

The Communist Threat   117

In God We Trust   125

Operation Northwoods   130

The Second Successful American Coup d'état: The JFK
    Assassination   135

1964: The Gulf of Tonkin Deception   145

The Assassinations of MLK and RFK: The Third Successful
    Coup d'état in American History   148

The Stock Market Casino: A Bubble Waiting to Happen   166

The New Silk Road Led Right to 9/11   171

1999: The Repeal of the Glass-Steagall Act   175

9/11   176

Recent Secret History   195

Current Secret History   200

Endnotes   *202*

Part One:

Background

The Spanish Menace ... The Red Menace ... The Axis of Evil: Convenient Menaces to Justify War

I n 1898, a majority of American citizens were convinced that Spaniards were inherently evil. In possibly the first actual instance of "fake news," yellow journalism utilized sensationalism, opinionated exaggeration, and eye-catching headlines to sell millions of newspapers and paint Spain as an international menace. Following the loss of 260 US servicemen killed in an explosion on the USS *Maine*, which sank while docked in the Havana, Cuba harbor, President McKinley and Congress declared war on the European nation. Within a matter of weeks, the United States acquired Cuba, Guam, Puerto Rico, Hawaii, and the Philippines, where almost 250,000 Filipinos perished while fighting the American occupation for three years.

Just one year after the end of the Filipino War, Chauncey Depew, general counsel of the Vanderbilt Railroad, president of the New York Central Railroad, and a United States Senator, stated at the 1904 Republican National Convention:

> The American people now produce $2 billion worth more than they can consume and we have met the emergency, and by the providence of God, by the statesmanship of William McKinley, and by the valor of Roosevelt and his associates, we have our market in Cuba . . . in Puerto Rico, in Hawaii . . . in the Philippines,

and we stand in the presence of 800 million people, with the Pacific as an American lake, and the American artisans producing better and cheaper goods than any country in the world. . . . Let production go on . . . let the factories do their best, let labor be employed at the highest wages, because the world is ours.[1]

Two hundred sixty American sailors had perished just six years prior, a quarter-million Filipinos had died defending their homeland, but the US government had markets for its $2 billion surplus exports, and thanks to God, President McKinley, and Roosevelt and his associates, *the world was ours.*

★

Many Americans have lived and died under the threat of the Communist menace. The Korean and Vietnamese Wars, and the ensuing Cambodian and Laotian conflicts killed around 100,000 Americans, injured and maimed hundreds of thousands of its soldiers, and killed and maimed millions of local militia and inhabitants. The toll on America's national debt was staggering, and, in the case of Vietnam, America's social and moral consciousness was ripped apart. All for what—this communist menace? The Vietnam War ended in 1975, yet a mere seventeen years later in 1992, the United States government and Hanoi began trading with one another, currently exporting and importing billions of dollars of merchandise each year.

And those feared Russian and Chinese commie dogs? According to the 2017 Hurun Global Rich List, China now has more billionaires than any country in the world with 609, followed by the US with 552, while Russia boasts 68![2] New York has a professional basketball team—the Brooklyn Nets—owned by one of those Russian billionaires until owner Mikhail Prokhorov sold it in late 2019 for $3.5 billion to Taiwanese billionaire Joe Tsai. The Berlin Wall fell in 1989, and in 2009, a "Communist" purchased a US sports franchise (the seventh most valuable NBA team) *and* its home—the Barclay Center in downtown Brooklyn, valued at $1.8 billion in December 2017.[3] Just a little over twenty years prior, Americans were programmed to fear a Soviet Union nuclear attack, but now those same people run an NBA team. That Commie menace has since been replaced by the terrorist menace, which has justified more wars, this time in Afghanistan and Iraq, and additional incursions into other Middle Eastern and African nations.

Most Americans remember President George W. Bush's axis of evil. The United States had just come out of one of the most profitable and peaceful decades in its history. On September 12, 2001, nothing in the world had changed but for a horrific act committed the day before by a maniacal terrorist group that desperately needed to be stopped from ever performing such a heinous and treacherous deed ever again, anywhere on the face of the Earth. Yet suddenly, the president of the United States, the so-called leader of the free world, was calling for a war against an "axis of evil"—Iran, Iraq, and North Korea. Forget containing the Red Menace; now the United States and its allies were going to fight evil.

What's wrong here? Doesn't it seem that every major event in the last half century has been distorted, most often to justify the deployment of American troops? Believe it or not, the United States has been at war for roughly 40 of the last 120 years, almost always accompanied by an imaginary menace. America's men and women have been sent into battle an average of once every three years since 1898, and the amount of wealth and strategic power gained from these wars is staggering. When you think about it, though, this makes a whole lot of sense, all boiling down to control—economic control. If America doesn't control an industry or a strategic area or a natural resource (like, maybe, oil), then someone else will. Russia? China? A friendly ally?

Although the 1800s were certainly a preamble, real American economic history effectively skyrocketed in the early 1900s. The 1913 passing of the Sixteenth Amendment allowed the IRS to begin collecting a federal income tax. The wealthiest Americans—among them the so-called robber barons of the nineteenth century—in apparent collusion with the US Congress, arranged for charitable contributions to be deducted from gross incomes. This allowed vastly wealthy individuals to place a substantial portion of their fortunes in IRS-untouchable nonprofit foundations exempt from 7 percent taxation. Two of the most notable are the Carnegie Foundation (chartered in 1906) and the Rockefeller Foundation (1913). These foundations not only provided tax shelters for fortunes but created think tanks that would form policy and tactics for even further gains in wealth and influence (as you'll learn in the next chapter).

It should be noted here that Congress's passing of the Tax Reform Bill in 2017, beginning with 2018 taxes, lists the charitable deduction as one of the few remaining deductions still available for taxpayers to itemize. It is no surprise that not only did Congress retain this all-important tax deduction for the ultra-wealthy to protect a good portion of their income as tax-free, but also that they knew to do it. Ironically, since fewer middle and lower-class Americans will most likely not itemize beginning in 2018 due to the eradication of most of their previous deductions and the corresponding increase of their standard deductions, many taxpayers possibly will discontinue contributing to worthwhile nonprofit organizations.

Although the 1898 Spanish-American War was a global affair, with the United States assimilating additional territory spanning two oceans, the people of the United States generally had only one concern—the freedom of the people of Cuba. Isolationist by nature, as our forefathers desired, the average American citizen simply wanted to stay out of the affairs of other countries. Having formed their wealthy and powerful trusts in the early 1900s to avoid their tax burden, the American economic elite presumably had another agenda. And as will be seen, two of those agendas were the control of the American education system and the US State Department.

Was This the Beginning of the Deep State?

In 1953, the House of Representatives' Cox Committee was re-formed into the Reece Committee, established by House Resolution 561 of the 82nd Congress to investigate whether tax-exempt organizations were using their funds to support communism. Banker Norman Dodd was selected to lead the investigation and accepted the consultancy as research director for the House of Representatives Special Committee to Investigate Tax-Exempt Foundations and Comparable Organizations. The chairman of this panel was Representative Carroll Reece (R-TN) who decided to focus on the twelve largest foundations (Rockefeller, Ford, Carnegie, etc.) since they represented 70 percent of the assets of all foundations at that time. Rene Wormser was hired as counsel on September 1, 1953, and Dodd hired, among others, attorney Kathryn Casey as a legal analyst.

Wormser was the senior member of the law firm of Myles, Wormser, & Koch, and a first-hand witness to the intense and powerful opposition to this investigation by these multi-billion-dollar trusts. The committee members were virtually hamstrung from the beginning of the investigation. In his 1958 book *Foundations: Their Power and Influence*, Wormser states:

An unparalleled amount of power is concentrated increasingly in the hands of an interlocking and self-perpetuating group. Unlike the power of corporate management, it is unchecked by stockholders; unlike the power of government, it is unchecked by the people; unlike the power of churches, it is unchecked by any firmly established canons of value.[4]

. . . When such foundations do good, they justify the tax-exempt status which the people grant them. When they do harm, it can be immense harm—there is virtually no counterforce to oppose them.[5]

According to the Dodd Report, the committee was to investigate whether the foundations had used their resources for purposes contrary to those for which they were established:

- As Un-American?
- Subversive?
- Political purposes?
- Resorted to propaganda in order to achieve the objectives for which they have made grants?

Dodd further stated, "To insure these determinations being made on the basis of impersonal facts, I directed the staff to make a study of the development of American Education since the turn of the century and of the trends and techniques of teaching and of the development of curricula since that time."[6]

It should be noted that on page five of Dodd's final report, he states, "As this report will hereafter contain many statements which appear to be conclusive, I emphasize here that each one of them must be understood to have resulted from studies which were essentially exploratory. In no sense should they be considered proved. I mention this in order to avoid the necessity of qualifying each as made."

It is also critical to point out, though, that there is no refuting the facts presented in both the interviews of Norman Dodd and the committee's final report, and that these findings are the direct result of a professionally conducted congressional committee and part of the congressional record for well over a half century. The report's conclusion states, "It seems incredible that the trustees of typically American fortune-created foundations should have permitted them to be used to finance ideas and practices incompatible with the fundamental concepts of our Constitution. Yet there seems evidence that this may have occurred."

Dodd began his investigation by sending the twelve largest foundations a letter, which included a list of specific questions. He soon received a response from Dr. Joseph Johnson, the recently appointed president of the Carnegie Endowment for International Peace (CEIP). A meeting with Johnson, Dodd, and the CEIP counsel was arranged. Johnson proceeded to tell Dodd that it would be almost impossible to answer the questions since all their pre–World War II records had been warehoused, as they were scheduled to move into new headquarters. Johnson offered to have the CEIP minutes made available to the committee in the CEIP library. Dodd promptly accepted and instructed attorney Kathryn Casey to concentrate on the years 1910 to 1920. Casey was perfect for the job as she saw no reason to criticize the foundations and no need for the committee investigation. Apparently, the foundation's new president had no idea of the incriminating evidence that was contained in those minutes. Shocked, Casey returned with findings that proved frightening.

William H. McIlhany II conducted an extensive interview with Norman Dodd for his 1980 book *The Tax-Exempt Foundations*. From McIlhany's interview transcript:

> [In the minutes, about 1911] the trustees raised a question. And they discussed the question and the question was specific, "Is there any means known to man more effective than war, assuming you wish to alter the life of an entire people? And they discussed this and at the end of a year they came to the conclusion that there was no more effective means to that end known to man. So, then they raised question number two, and the question was, "How do we involve the United States in a war?"[7]

And then they raised the question, "How do we control the diplomatic machinery of the United States?" And the answer came out, "We must control the State Department. . . ."[8]

To summarize Dodd's subsequent comments:[9]

- Every high appointment in the State Department was to be cleared through an agency that the CEIP set up. [S. H. Note: Was this the beginning of the nation's most influential policy-making think tank—the Council on Foreign Relations?] From the early 1900s, high appointees to each president's State Department, responsible for America's foreign policy, were apparently cleared by a 501c tax-exempt *private* foundation.
- Upon the United States entry into World War I, these same trustees in a meeting in 1917 congratulated themselves on the wisdom of their original decision, because already the impact of war had indicated it would—and can—alter life in this country. They even had the audacity to dispatch a telegram to President Wilson, *cautioning him to see that the war did not end too quickly*. [Italics inserted by S. H. to add emphasis.]
- The war was now over. Then the concern became, as expressed by the trustees, seeing to it that there was no reversion to life in this country as it existed prior to 1914. And they came to the conclusion that, *to prevent a reversion, they must control education*. [Italics inserted by S. H. to add emphasis.]
- Approaching the Rockefeller Foundation, the CEIP (Carnegie Foundation) asked, "Will you take on the acquisition of control of education as it involves subjects that are domestic in their significance? We'll take it on the basis of subjects that have an international significance."
- The trustees then decided that the key to controlling education is the teaching of American history, but they were unsuccessful in getting historians to commit to this. The Guggenheim, though, agreed to grant scholarships to selected candidates who were going on to graduate degrees. And so it began.

As McIlhany points out next, "Not only did some of America's most respected historians swallow the line that Germany was completely responsible for World War I, but . . . [the CEIP] organized the National Board for Historical Service which was designed to line up all the historians in the Allied cause and in support of Wilson's interventionist policies."[10] World War I was actually started by Austria-Hungary declaring war on Serbia, with countries aligned in treaties with the two countries joining. Germany entered on the side of Austria-Hungary.

Dodd directed his staff to explore foundation practices, educational procedures, and the operations of the executive branch of the federal government since 1903 for reasonable evidence of a purposeful relationship between them. Its ensuing studies disclosed such a relationship, and that it had existed continuously since the beginning of this fifty-year period. In addition, these studies seem to give evidence of a response to our involvement in international affairs. Grants had been made by foundations (chiefly by Carnegie and Rockefeller) which were used to further this purpose by:

- Directing education in the United States toward an international viewpoint and discrediting the traditions to which it had been dedicated.
- Training individuals and servicing agencies to render advice to the executive branch of the federal government.
- Decreasing the dependency of education upon the resources of the local community and freeing it from many of the natural safeguards inherent in this American tradition.
- Changing both school and college curricula to the point where they sometimes denied the principles underlying the American way of life.
- Financing experiments designed to determine the most effective means by which education could be pressed into service of a political nature.

Dodd realized that the committee had to study the development of American education since the turn of the century, including the trends of techniques of teaching and the curriculum, so he directed his staff to investigate the following agencies where the developments and trends had been traced: the American Council of Learned Societies, the Social Science Research Council, the American Council on Education, the National Education Association, the League for Industrial Democracy, the Progressive Education Association, the American Historical Association, the John Dewey Society, the Anti-Defamation League, and the National Research Council.

After identifying the above foundation-funded groups, Dodd stated that his investigation "has revealed not only their support by foundations but has disclosed a degree of cooperation between them which they have referred to as 'an interlock,' thus indicating a concentration of influence and power. By this phrase they indicate they are bound by a common interest rather than a dependency upon a single source for capital funds. It is difficult to study their relationship without confirming this. Likewise, it is difficult to avoid the feeling that their common interest . . . *lies in the planning and control of certain aspects of American life through a combination of the federal government and education.*"[11] [Italics inserted by S. H. to add emphasis.]

Other significant observations from the final report:

- "Some of the larger foundations have directly supported 'subversion' in the true meaning of that term—namely, the process of undermining some of our vitally protective concepts and principles. They have actively supported attacks upon our social and governmental system and financed the promotion of socialism and collectivist ideas."

- "In summary: Our study of these entities and their relationship to each other seems to warrant the inference that they constitute a highly efficient, functioning whole. Its product is apparently *an educational curriculum designed to indoctrinate the American student* from matriculation to the consummation of his education. It contrasts sharply with the freedom of the individual as the cornerstone of our social structure. For this freedom, it seems to substitute the group, the will of the majority, and a centralized power to enforce this will—presumably in the interest of all." [Italics inserted by S. H. to add emphasis.]

- "The result of this network in which Foundations have played such a significant role seems to have provided this country with what is tantamount to a national system of education under the tight control of organizations and persons little known to the American public."

- "Principles and their truth or falsity seem to have concerned them very little."

- "In what appears from our studies to have been zeal for a radically new social order in the United States, many of these social science *specialists apparently gave little thought to either the opinions or the warnings of those who were convinced that a wholesale acceptance of knowledge acquired almost entirely by empirical methods would result in a deterioration of moral standards and a disrespect for principles. Even past experience which indicated that such an approach to the problems of society could lead to tyranny, appears to have been disregarded.*" [Italics inserted by S. H. to add emphasis.]

The latter point deserves further thought. Though President Donald Trump's political base seems to be solidly behind him, certainly representing a very large percentage of the country's voice, his political foes lend credence to the belief that many of the administration's policies reflect an unrestrained exercise of power. Sixty-four years earlier, did Norman Dodd's final report to the Reese Committee's Congressional investigation of tax-exempt foundations contain a foreboding warning?

In conclusion, presumably charitable and philanthropical foundations sought to control your and your ancestors' education, requested that the president of the United States unnecessarily continue to keep our soldiers in harm's way, and directed the presidential cabinet responsible for American foreign policy. Singling out the Ford Foundation, Dodd notes, "It is significant that the policies of this foundation include making funds available for certain aspects of secret military research and for the education of the Armed Forces. It becomes even more significant when it is realized that the responsibility for the selection of the personnel engaged in these projects is known to rest on the foundation itself—subject as it may be to screening by our military authorities."[12]

Not surprisingly, a report revealing that nonprofit foundations were controlling US education and our State Department, and instigating internationalism and collectivism, did not sit too well within certain government circles. The attacks came from both liberal and conservative influences, including the *New York Times*. The committee was quickly dissolved, and the report quietly banished to the congressional file room.

As McIlhany says, "Under the weight of media and, possibly, White House pressure . . . the minority report submitted by Hays and Pfost was a masterpiece of self-righteous indignation that depended for its credibility on the fact that most of those who read it or media reports of its contents had read none of the hearings. . . . Perhaps the most revealing fact about the frightened elite's attack on the Reece Committee was their frantic effort to discredit or belittle the witnesses who testified against them as men . . . 'of dubious standing.'"[13] As McIlhany's notes show, "Reece managed to answer the few specific things Hutchins had actually said, including the fact that the witnesses 'of dubious standing' had been faculty members of Columbia University, Yale University, Harvard University, Northwestern University, and the University of Pennsylvania."[14]

Between May 10 and July 9, 1954, the Reece Committee on Tax-Exempt Foundations produced 2,086 pages of testimony. On June 3, Assistant Research Director Thomas M. McNiece made his presentation before the committee, and it clearly shows how deep the foundation reach went into American life. From the June 3rd transcript:

McNiece presented the following chart which he headed, "Inter-Relationships Between Foundations, Education, and Government," and in which he said, "This chart as a whole will be useful in locating the areas in which we have found evidence of questionable procedure against what we deem to be public interest . . ."[15]

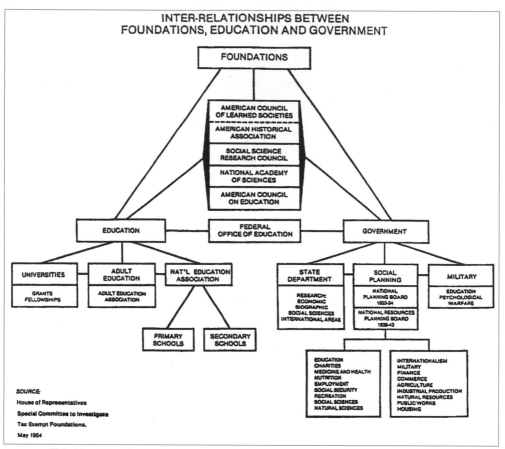

INTER-RELATIONSHIPS BETWEEN FOUNDATIONS, EDUCATION AND GOVERNMENT

FOUNDATIONS

AMERICAN COUNCIL OF LEARNED SOCIETIES

AMERICAN HISTORICAL ASSOCIATION

SOCIAL SCIENCE RESEARCH COUNCIL

NATIONAL ACADEMY OF SCIENCES

AMERICAN COUNCIL ON EDUCATION

EDUCATION — **FEDERAL OFFICE OF EDUCATION** — **GOVERNMENT**

UNIVERSITIES — **ADULT EDUCATION** — **NAT'L EDUCATION ASSOCIATION**

GRANTS FELLOWSHIPS

ADULT EDUCATION ASSOCIATION

PRIMARY SCHOOLS — SECONDARY SCHOOLS

STATE DEPARTMENT — **SOCIAL PLANNING** — **MILITARY**

RESEARCH: ECONOMIC BIOGRAPHIC SOCIAL SCIENCES INTERNATIONAL AREAS

NATIONAL PLANNING BOARD 1933-34

NATIONAL RESOURCES PLANNING BOARD 1939-43

EDUCATION PSYCHOLOGICAL WARFARE

EDUCATION
CHARITIES
MEDICINE AND HEALTH
NUTRITION
EMPLOYMENT
SOCIAL SECURITY
RECREATION
SOCIAL SCIENCES
NATURAL SCIENCES

INTERNATIONALISM
MILITARY
FINANCE
COMMERCE
AGRICULTURE
INDUSTRIAL PRODUCTION
NATURAL RESOURCES
PUBLIC WORKS
HOUSING

SOURCE:
House of Representatives
Special Committee to Investigate
Tax Exempt Foundations.
May 1954

This May 1954 Congressional Committee chart tracks the flow of money, men, and ideas from the tax-exempt foundations into critical sectors of American life.

The ensuing financial data will give some idea of the great amount of funds and their distribution made, available in the educational field by a few of the larger foundations. The statement is by no means complete. In fact it contains the contributions of only six of the larger foundations where the specific beneficiaries are named. These six are as follows: The Carnegie Corporation of New York, The Carnegie Endowment for International Peace, The Carnegie Foundation for the Advancement of Teaching, The Rockefeller Foundation, The General Education Board, [and] The Ford Foundation (two instances only). . . .

McNiece then listed the following associations and the grant amounts that each has received from the above six foundations totaling over $60 million: American Council on Education, American Historical Association, American Council of Learned Societies, Council on Foreign Relations, Foreign Policy Association, Institute of International Education, Institute of Pacific Relations, National Academy of Sciences (including National Research Council), National Education Association, Progressive Education Association, Social Science Research Council.

> Great benefit has unquestionably resulted to all mankind from the contributions of these and other foundations and there is no intention to gainsay or minimize this or to detract from the credit due the foundations for these benefits . . . What this investigation does seem to indicate is that many small grants have found their way into questionable hands and many large ones in points of concentrated use have been devoted to purposes that are promoting a departure from the fundamental concepts of education and government under our Constitution. *That this may be recognized by those engaged in such activities is indicated by the frequent references in their own literature to the "age of transition" through which we are passing, and the responsibility that must be assumed by educators in leading the way. No one in full possession of his faculties should oppose change for the better but change for the sake of change alone may prove to be a dangerous delusion.* . . . [Italics inserted by S. H. to add emphasis.]
>
> According to our compilations, the Carnegie Corp. has contributed to all educational purposes, from 1911 to 1950, approximately $25,300,000 . . . from 1902 to 1951, the Rockefeller Foundation and the General Education Board combined to universities and including only the totals to the ten largest beneficiaries of each of the two foundations in each State of the United States contributed over $290 million. . . ."
>
> "We find that the responsibilities of the leaders and teachers in the world of education are especially emphasized during

this age of transition, as demonstrated in the final report, 16th volume, of the Commission on Social Studies as previously quoted on page 15. In the mid-forties, the president appointed a Commission on Higher Education. Their conclusions and recommendations were reported in a series of six pamphlets in December 1947. Mr. George F. Zook, president of the American Council of Learned Societies, was chairman of this Commission. In the Commission's reports they gave credit to the following organizations for aid received: American Council of Learned Societies, American Council on Education, National Research Council, Social Science Research Council, American Association of University Professors, and Association of Land Grant Colleges and Universities. The following quotations are taken from the pages indicated in volume I of the Report of the President's Commission on Higher Education Page 6: Education: Perhaps its most important role is to serve as *an instrument of social transition, and its responsibilities are defined in terms of the kind of civilization society hopes to build.* Page 84: *Higher education must be alert to anticipate new social and economic needs, and to keep its programs of professional training in step with the requirements of a changing and expanding cultural, social, and economic order. . . .*"[16] [Italics inserted by S. H. to add emphasis.]

Americans presumably send their children to school to learn English grammar and spelling, foreign languages, arithmetic, American and World history, science, etc. The nonprofit and tax-exempt foundations apparently have other visions of educating America's children: Collectivism. Internationalism. Social transition. Age of transition.

The Myth and Deception
of American Democracy

How do you get Americans to believe that they are controlling their destiny, that they live in a democracy where their votes count, and whatever happens, good or bad, they—the citizenry—are the catalyst because they voted for those politicians, for those amendments, for those laws?

The answer—a two-party system with seemingly polarizing objectives. For instance, from very soon after the foundations established themselves, the Republican Party has stood for high defense spending and the Democrats for big government spending, with both acting as war chiefs when the time was ripe for American troops to be led into battle.

Left-wing (Democratic) abortion rights, same-sex marriage, gun control, protection for immigrants; versus right-wing (Republican), pro-life, the sanctity of marriage, gun rights, religious freedom, a wall across our southern border—all a polarizing mechanism to keep the populace fighting amongst itself, believing that they have succeeded or failed at these social values with their votes and elected politicians.

One simply must look at a September 2014 CNN/ORC poll that showed that 65 percent of Americans think the current Congress is the worst in their lifetime.[17] It is staggering that two out of three Americans view the 535 legislators they voted for only a few years ago as the very worst. Or, consider a November 2015 report by the Pew

17

Research Center that states only 19 percent of Americans trust the government always or most of the time.[18] Four out of five voters not trusting the government that they voted for is representative of the myth and deception of American democracy.

For decades, members of Congress have voted or failed to vote on what is important to them and their party affiliations, not to their constituents who voted them into office, making it quite obvious that voters are not in control of their democratic destiny at all. A Gallup poll released on November 9, 2017 (two days after President Trump was elected), reported that 51 percent of Americans were in favor of increased gun legislation.[19] *PolitiFact* reported in 2015 that 74 percent of National Rifle Association members support requiring background checks for all gun sales, and a June 2017 Quinnipiac University poll showed that 94 percent of all Americans support background checks for all gun buyers. Yet according to the *Washington Examiner* on October 3, 2017, Republicans were nowhere near favoring gun control legislation even after 59 people were killed in the Las Vegas massacre.[20]

Once again, politicians voted into office by their constituents to vote for what those constituents want and need, voted along party lines to satisfy a lobby that helped get them into office, and probably most importantly, will almost certainly keep them in office if they wish to stay there. What almost every voter forgets is that they are simply the end result of the voting process. They are essentially given the opportunity to vote for the two candidates selected by those two parties. Yes, citizens can point to the fact that in a presidential election, they choose the candidate via the primary process; however, by and large, those primary candidates have already been chosen as potential presidential material. It matters little who or which party wins. The victory is in seeing every American believe that they are part of the system when they are simply observers, while their legislators vote along party lines and for personal profit. Is it any wonder that four out of five Americans, in supposedly the greatest democracy of all time, don't trust the government always or most of the time?

When US citizens cast their vote for president and vice president, they are voting for their electors within the country's Electoral

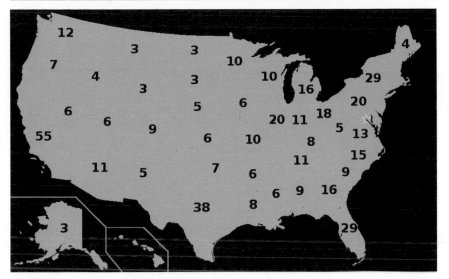

Electoral college map for the 2012, 2016, and 2020 United States presidential elections, using apportionment data released by the US Census Bureau. Original: Cg-Realms, Derivative: Ali Zifan, 2013.

College—*not* for the individuals. Though many Americans understand this, what too many aren't aware of is that these electors are morally and ethically bound to vote for their party's candidates, but *not* legally. Theoretically, every voter in your state can vote for the Republican candidate for president; yet any or all of your state's "faithless electors" can vote for the Democratic candidate if they so choose, and vice versa of course. This is a disaster just waiting to happen.

And it has other meaningful ramifications as well. The Electoral College ensures that the more liberal, progressive, and moderate states—generally large populated areas such as New York, California, Pennsylvania, and Illinois—don't sway the popular vote during presidential elections away from the more conservative smaller states such as New Mexico, Kansas, and Idaho. In this manner, the African-American and Hispanic minority voters—and third-party candidates—are almost totally neutralized. Most Americans are aware that both Republican Presidents George W. Bush and Donald Trump lost the popular vote by 543,895 and nearly 3 million votes, respectively.

Freedom of the press is another American democratic myth. Sure, the media is free to print any story it wants; however, what does and does not get printed isn't determined by the government, as dictator-ships are, but by the media moguls and the established set of rules that trickle down to the editors who must abide (much more about this in "So You Heard About All This on TV and in the Newspapers, Huh?" chapter).

Believe it or not, prior to 2012, insider trading was not against the law for members of Congress. So, any information they discovered while in elective office, they were free to use in their personal invest-ments. Ratted out by *60 Minutes* on November 13, 2011, Congress was forced in 2012 to enact the Stock Act, which made them liable to the same insider trading laws as everyone else. But they would have none of that. Just one year later, in 2013, your elected officials in the Senate and the House voted and fast-tracked a new law excising large sections of the Stock Act. Specifically, congressional staffers no longer have to disclose their financial transactions publicly, and it has been made almost impossible for anyone to inspect the database of 2,900 congressional staffers to see if anyone is breaking the law.[21]

- Whereas it easily could take years to pass legislation for tax-payer jobs, healthcare, social security benefits, etc., it report-edly took the Senate less than a day to unanimously pass the bill after many members had already gone home (a la the pas-sage of the Federal Reserve Act in 1913, which you'll learn about later).
- The next day, it went to the House where it reportedly passed in thirty seconds.
- No sooner was the ink dry on the passage of the House bill, that it went to the Oval Office where another elected official, President of the United States Barack Obama, promptly signed it into law where it now stands.[22]

Lobbyists, defined by dictionary.com as "people who attempt to influ-ence legislation on behalf of a special interest," are another means that reflect the myth and deception of American democracy. Citizens elect their representatives based on their ideals, how they want their com-munity to be represented, how they wish their health care, retirement, living conditions, etc. to be monitored and made better; yet lobbyists such as Planned Parenthood, the NRA, and all the other organizations can use their power to influence representatives. Whereas citizens should hold the power with their elected officials, it's the lobbyists who are some of the most powerful men, women, and organizations in Washington.

Though the effects of the Citizens United Supreme Court ruling in 2010 will be covered extensively later, it should be pointed out here that because of the ruling, corporations (and unions) can now legally spend millions of dollars in order to convince voters to vote for or against all candidates and political parties who will potentially increase their profits. In other words, voters can donate $5 or $100 or $1000 for a candidate, but corporations and unions acting as lobbyists can spend millions on advertising for candidates and parties that will almost certainly support their needs.

On June 12, 2016, forty-nine people were killed and fifty-three injured in one of the largest mass shootings in the history of the United States. Just three days later, Donald Trump tweeted, "I will be meeting with the NRA, who has endorsed me, about not allowing people on the terrorist watch list, or the no fly list, to buy guns." A presidential candidate, who ultimately did become president of the United States, felt a need to ask an organization that endorsed him if he could change his party's platform to support a change in American gun laws that could potentially save American lives.

This is the power that lobbies have; this is where American democracy has moved from "for the people" to "for the lobbyist, including corporate profits."

So You Heard about All This on TV and in the Newspapers, Huh?

Why has the media in the last century not reported many of the facts contained in *real* American history? To understand this, one must first understand the mindset of the American media. They are not investigative by nature, and generally report what they believe the public wants to hear. Official stories are easy, with facts that don't require verification. Without Deep Throat leading Woodward and Bernstein from one source to another, Watergate would have been buried, President Nixon would have victoriously finished his two terms in office, and Dustin Hoffman and Robert Redford would have had one less movie to their credit.

A story on the Federal Reserve System or any other act that strays from the official story requires official sources to come forward, "spilling the beans." The famous investigative TV series *60 Minutes* is more than free by CBS executives to rat out the tobacco or meat industry, report on a military scandal or the like, or as we've already shown, expose Congress for engaging in insider trading for decades. Yet this highly acclaimed investigative news team, on the air for almost half a century, has not reported on the abundance of ballistic and autopsy reports, and firsthand accounts, that significantly detract from the official story that Sirhan B. Sirhan was a lone gunman; nearly an impossibility that he assassinated arguably the next president of the United States (more on this later in "The Assassinations of MLK and RFK"). Media giants have a structure of news reporting that has been determined by their owners. Reporters have their stories filtered through this tightly-knit structure, and if it doesn't fit, it's out.

Furthermore, stories are generally assigned by the editors, rather than vice versa. How many articles have you read in newspapers that contain the byline "AP"? The Associated Press is a not-for-profit cooperative owned by American newspapers and broadcasters. Much of your news, both print and via the airwaves, is controlled by the AP. Control the AP, and you control the news that reaches a billion people in 120 countries.

Vincent Bugliosi (1934–2015), arguably one of the most acclaimed trial lawyers in the history of our country, was the winner of three Edgar Allan Poe Awards (the top honor for crime writers) and had three number-one true crime bestsellers. His book *The Prosecution of George W. Bush for Murder*, published by Vanguard Press (then a member of the Perseus Group, now part of the Hachette Book Group), is quite possibly one of the biggest examples of literary manipulation of the media that this country has ever seen. It's the perfect example of how the news networks and the talk shows introduce you only to the voices, opinions, and news stories that they wish to promote.

Bugliosi, who never lost a case as a prosecutor and defense attorney, argues quite convincingly that the president of the United States took the country into war under false pretenses, and as such, should be tried for murder for the four thousand-plus deaths of American soldiers in Iraq. The key here, though, is not whether former president Bush is guilty or not guilty—in this country, a person is innocent until proven otherwise—it's that Bugliosi has presented a legal premise of sufficient evidence to not only possibly impeach (bring to trial before Congress), but to try Bush for murder in courts of law in each of the fifty states where a citizen soldier has been killed. And except for a few rare appearances such as *Book Talk* on CSPAN, the media never informed the nation and the world of Bugliosi's evidence. No, not even *60 Minutes*.

Opponents might argue that the presidency is the office, and not a man or woman, yet that meant nothing to Congress and the media when it came to tearing the presidency apart for approximately two years by impeaching Bill Clinton for lying about a consensual extra-marital affair. With just a whimper of publicity, the book sold moderately well, bolstered by the Internet and some 100 radio interviews. But of the approximately 160 million Americans of voting age, only a fraction knew the book and the thesis existed, because the mainstream media gave it very little attention.

Another even more powerful example of the American people being manipulated and controlled by the media is one that involves President Ronald Reagan, then–vice president George H. W. Bush, and John Hinckley, Jr. Hinckley had fired several shots at Reagan in 1981, injuring several people including the president. In covering the story, the *Houston Post* and NBC News anchor John Chancellor reported that Hinckley's brother, Scott, was an acquaintance of Neil Bush, the son of the vice president—the man who would have assumed the most powerful office in the world had Hinckley's bullet been roughly half an inch closer to Reagan's heart.[23] As a matter of fact, Neil and Scott were scheduled to have dinner at the Bush home the night after the shooting. But wouldn't you know, the story vanished from the media, never reported again by CBS, ABC, the *New York Times, Washington Post*, or any other media outlet, except for a buried mention in the April 13, 1981, issue of *Newsweek*, on page 59.[24]

Nathaniel Blumberg, Rhodes Scholar and former professor at the University of Montana School of Journalism, is the author of the self-published *The Afternoon of March 30*, a novel that takes the facts he has gathered and presents them as fiction. His purpose was not to suggest that there was a conspiracy to assassinate Reagan; rather that there was a conspiracy to prevent powerful information from reaching the public—information that every citizen should have had the opportunity to hear.[25]

Neil Bush had told reporters in Denver that he had met Scott at a surprise party in the Bush home a couple of months prior to the assassination attempt, and according to one newspaper, the Bush and Hinckley families had social ties. Scott Hinckley's oil business, Vanderbilt Energy Corporation, had been audited, and a pricing violation on sales of crude oil between 1977 and 1980 was discovered that could have earned penalties amounting to $2,000,000 by the US

A montage of the Reagan assassination attempt. Photos courtesy of the Ronald Reagan Library, 1981.

1. President Reagan waves to crowd immediately before being shot.
2. Shots have been fired. The president is in the limousine to the right. Guards move in on the gunman.
3. Secret Service agents join the commotion while other people take cover.
4. Washington, D.C. police officer Thomas Delahanty (foreground) and Press Secretary James Brady (behind) lie wounded on the ground. Two Secret Service agents reach for what appears to be the gun that had been fired.

Department of Energy. In a meeting that broke up just an hour prior to the shooting, Scott requested some time to come up with an explanation as to how this happened.[26]

Ralph W. McGehee, author of *Deadly Deceits: My 25 Years in the CIA*, reviewed the novel and said it "epitomizes how our government serves the mighty and uses the trumped-up excuse of national security to trample our freedoms . . ." and helps "to understand the powerful forces controlling if not destroying our country." Theresa Walla of United Press International interviewed Blumberg, and her story was distributed on March 9, 1985, by Helena UPI. Interestingly, the Seattle UPI bureau asked for a longer and more detailed piece, which Walla sent them. This expanded article was then sent by to the national UPI desk, where it was killed.[27] Just one more example that America's free press is certainly free to print any bit of news that it wants, but that it also censors whatever news the media moguls deem unnecessary for the public to see.

And would you believe there's more? The judge presiding at John

Hinckley's trial was Barrington D. Parker. And in 2001, very soon after assuming office, President George W. Bush appointed Parker's son as a Federal Appeals Court judge. Parker Jr. was subsequently unanimously approved by the Senate.

FBI photo of disassembled fireworks, which were recovered from a backpack inside a trash bag in a landfill near University of Massachusetts–Dartmouth campus. In an affidavit, the FBI alleges friends of the suspected marathon bomber Dzhokhar Tsarnaev found the backpack and attempted to dispose of it for him. FBI, 2013.

And then there's the horrific Boston Marathon bombing. I am not saying that Dzhokhar and Tamerlan Tsarnaev were not guilty. The brothers certainly may have committed those heinous acts of terrorism, murder, and dismemberment. But let's study the "official story," and look at the holes that have never been questioned by the mainstream media. And that's very important—*never questioned*. There has been at least one book and several newspaper and magazine articles, that have purported that Tamerlan Tsarnaev made several trips to Russia prior to the bombing and that he may have been an FBI informant, but certainly that the FBI knew he was a potential jihadist. Daniel Morley, who had ties to Tamerlan, was found to have a stockpile of bomb-making components in his bedroom, possibly indicating that the Tsarnaevs did not make the two bombs themselves. And if that is the case, why wasn't Morley prosecuted instead of being placed in three mental health facilities for two years? Why was he coincidentally released about a month after Dzhokhar Tsarnaev was sentenced to death, and why does he now have a state job driving a van which transports the elderly?[28] There is more:

- From the start, the FBI head in charge of the investigation publicly stated live on national television that no one should pay any attention to any marathon-related photos other than the official photos released by him. Did he perchance mean the photos online of the bomb-sniffing dogs at the *start* of the race? And why were they there in the first place? (This was corroborated by many of the runners and their family and friends.) What about the photos clearly showing known US government contractors near the finish line where the bombs were detonated, wearing backpacks almost identical to the ones allegedly used by the brothers?

- No one ever questioned why only one of the brothers wore sunglasses while they walked through the marathon crowds prior to the bombing. One would think that if they were smart enough to plan this horrific act, killing 3 and injuring 264 innocent victims, that they would either have worn disguises or would have at least been wearing sunglasses while passing by numerous video surveillance cameras on the way to their targets. The big question is, if they had, would they have been identified and caught?

- And speaking of that trek through the crowds, they sure as hell do not look like they are carrying backpacks filled with metal pressure cookers complete with nails and other deadly paraphernalia.

- A few days after the bombing, and presumably with the police having no idea of the location of the brothers, they allegedly killed Sean Collier of the MIT police department on their escape attempt from the Boston area. The officer was found dead, sitting in his patrol car with his gun in its holster. Why?

What was their motive for this seemingly senseless ambush? All it did was bring police attention to the area, and the brothers didn't even take his gun! No one, not one reporter, questioned that there was no reason for this senseless act.

- The Tsarnaevs then carjacked a Mercedes and kidnapped the driver, allowing him to escape so he could call 911 and again alert the police to not only their location, but their car and license plate! They had *allegedly* committed a terrorist attack against the United States of America and fatally shot a policeman moments before, so why didn't they simply put a hole in the driver's head, just as they did the MIT cop? If they had, they most likely would have been walking around Times Square a few days later, which is *allegedly* where they were headed to carry out further bombings. Instead, Tamerlan Tsarnaev died, and Dzhokhar Tsarnaev has been sentenced to death.

- Then there's the huge shootout between what seems like dozens of police and the brothers. Getting back into his SUV, Dzhokhar *allegedly* accidentally ran over his brother and drove away, not to be seen for hours until found hiding in a boat in someone's backyard. Not one newsperson questioned why the police didn't jump into their cruisers and chase Dzhokhar. Not one! True, it's been reported that Dzhokhar presumably ditched the Mercedes soon after leaving the shootout, but could a severely injured driver have eluded police cruisers if they had taken off after him immediately?

- And it gets even more bizarre. Dzhokhar Tsarnaev ditched the Mercedes around four blocks from where he was finally found in a boat, injured and covered by a tarp. We know he was injured prior because police found a pool of blood near the Mercedes. With no weapons, in total darkness in the middle of the night, and obviously bleeding, Dzhokhar Tsarnaev allegedly wrote a note in pencil on the side of the boat—approximately 225 words, which is a little less than a normal double-spaced typewritten page, basically stating that the USA is killing Muslims, that it must be punished for its crimes, and if you hurt one Muslim you hurt all Muslims. Tsarnaev could hardly stand when photographed being removed from the boat, was covered in blood, and had a bullet to his mouth. Might he have had other thoughts on his mind? Did he really have the ability to write all of that under those difficult circumstances, in almost total darkness and relatively neat handwriting?

Why didn't all the major network correspondents and interviewers ask these questions? The answer is that not only are they not allowed to question mainstream "official stories," they are like robots in reporting the news. They question nothing that is not mainstream and the official story, because that is the accepted established American media methodology. *Any variation from the official story is condemned as a conspiracy theory.* The Boston Marathon suspects may well have been guilty as charged. Dzhokhar Tsarnaev admitted in court to their complicity in the bombing. But we'll probably never know for sure, and almost certainly will never hear the answer to the questions posed above.

Never assume that the official story is accurate, or that there haven't been important pieces omitted. You must always second-guess, because the news media is controlled beyond the imagination.

Oh, and by the way, the Hinckley/Bush relationship was never reported on by *60 Minutes*.

From "Government of the People, by the People, for the People," To "Government of Big Business, by Big Business, for Big Business"

The Bosses of the Senate, a cartoon by Joseph Keppler. First published in *Puck* 1889. (This version published by the J. Ottmann Lith. Co.)

This frequently reproduced cartoon, long a staple of textbooks and studies of Congress, depicts corporate interests—from steel, copper, oil, iron, sugar, tin, and coal to paper bags, envelopes, and salt—as giant money bags looming over the tiny senators at their desks in the Chamber. A door to the gallery, the "people's entrance," is bolted and barred. The galleries stand empty while the special interests have floor privileges, operating below the motto: "This is the Senate of the Monopolists by the Monopolists and for the Monopolists!" Description from the website of the US Senate, 1889.

In 2013, there were approximately fifty to sixty countries around the world that offered foreigners safe tax havens with very little regulation and little or no taxation. The amount of money evading taxes was in the trillions.[29] US Fortune 500 companies keep $2.5 trillion offshore, avoiding three-quarters of a trillion dollars in Uncle Sam's revenue.[30] In 2014, Burger King acquired Canada's Tim Hortons, announcing that they will move their headquarters to Canada, costing the United States Treasury a lot of taxable income and job losses. In addition, Burger King will no longer be penalized with double taxation for its overseas earnings.[31]

This is just the tip of the iceberg when it comes to what globalization has done to American prosperity, livelihood, and its way of life. Proponents maintain that free trade opens up the world to great economic opportunities, including jobs, growth, and lower prices. Poor countries have a much better chance for improving their lot in life, and in the case of the United States, allows American companies new markets to sell their products, which in turn increases employment. In reality, for developed countries such as the United States, globalization is a drain on jobs and job income. Yes, technology including artificial intelligence has also had an adverse effect on the job market, but it is estimated that approximately two million US jobs have been lost to globalization since 1990.[32]

Americans, like other developed and industrialized countries, were blindly led into the notion that this is capitalism, and anything that has to do with free trade is a capitalistic blessing, and to be anti-globalism and anti–free trade is to be anti-American and a socialist. Nobody, especially presidents and congressmen, really gave any thought at all as to why American corporations should ever have been allowed to leave the country, how there were no restrictions placed on foreign ownership of our assets, how any American or corporation could be allowed to take US dollars abroad, and quite possibly the most egregious—how corporations can be allowed to keep their profits (cash) in countries where they made profits in order to avoid contributing their taxable income to Uncle Sam. For instance, Jeremy Owens of MarketWatch reported on January 27, 2016, that Apple has $200 billion in reserves overseas and does not plan on bringing the money back to the US, where it would then have to pay 40 percent in taxes.[33]

American workers don't give a damn about capitalism or socialism, but just being able to put food on the table and a roof over their heads. What led America and all the other industrialized countries astray is the behind-the-scenes shenanigans of big business and the completely *unrestricted* dalliances of these entities. Here are just a few examples:

The FDA: Big Pharma in conjunction with the FDA have brainwashed the country into believing that the only preventatives and cures are drugs. Yet, alternative medicine has been showing for decades that there are potentially natural preventative and healing vitamins, minerals, herbs, and foods. But the only accepted treatment for disease in the United States by the FDA, pharmaceutical companies, healthcare corporations, and the medical community, are drugs that make unimaginable profits for the pharmaceutical industry. In 2018, FDA Commissioner, Dr. Scott Gottlieb, had this to say on the FDA website: "FDA always faces big challenges because of where it sits at the intersection of so many critical concerns. By virtue of the fact that people's lives—quite literally—depend on what we do. Patient and consumer protection are at the heart of what we do. And I believe deeply in that fundamental mission of this agency." If people's lives are so important to the FDA, why haven't they established a Center For Natural Disease Control in order to perform extensive research on all of the potentially natural preventatives and cures for diseases that destroy people's lives and put their families at financial risk? It was reported in early 2016 that pharmaceutical companies spent $5.2 billion a year to advertise their drugs, with that number increasing every year.[34] Why is Big Pharm allowed such huge expenditures when it is doctors who prescribe the drugs? Many patients are financially suffering from the high cost of their drugs; Could this $5.2 billion have put a significant dent in their drug costs?

It shouldn't come as any surprise that the United States is the only industrialized country in the world with a for-profit private healthcare system rather than not-for-profit universal care. Take a look at these facts:

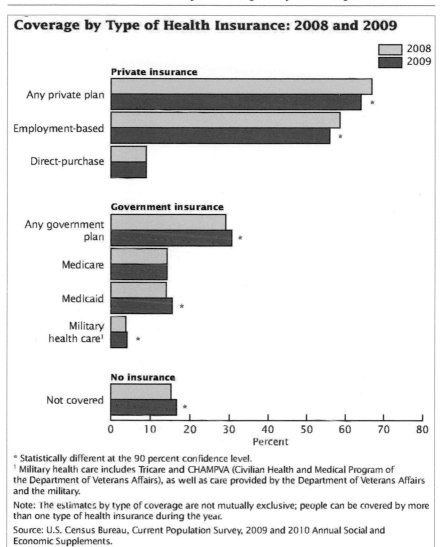

Coverage by Type of Health Insurance: 2008 and 2009

2008
2009

Private insurance

Any private plan
Employment-based
Direct-purchase

Government insurance

Any government plan
Medicare
Medicaid
Military health care[1]

No insurance

Not covered

Percent

* Statistically different at the 90 percent confidence level.
[1] Military health care includes Tricare and CHAMPVA (Civilian Health and Medical Program of the Department of Veterans Affairs), as well as care provided by the Department of Veterans Affairs and the military.

Note: The estimates by type of coverage are not mutually exclusive; people can be covered by more than one type of health insurance during the year.

Source: U.S. Census Bureau, Current Population Survey, 2009 and 2010 Annual Social and Economic Supplements.

Bar graph for the type of health insurance coverage (percentage) in 2008/2009 in the United States. DeNavas-Walt, Carmen, Bernadette D. Proctor, and Jessica C. Smith, US Census Bureau, 2010.

- In 2009, $200 million was paid to the top executives of the five largest for-profit health insurance companies in America.
- Aetna, Humana, United Healthcare, Cigna, Centene, and Anthem reaped a whopping $6 billion in profit *in the second quarter of 2017*, a 29 percent increase from the year before.[35] Pro-rated out, that's a $24 billion profit for the year!

- The biggest cause of a United States citizen declaring for
  bankruptcy is due to medical disasters and the ensuing medical expenses. In 2007, 62 percent of all personal bankruptcies
  was due to a medical problem, and 78 percent of those people
  actually had health insurance.[36] Big Pharma, doctors, and the
  healthcare companies make billions, and yet 78 percent of all
  personal bankruptcies had health insurance. Is it any wonder
  that the healthcare industry comprised of these three sectors is
  an annual multi-billion-dollar extravaganza where untold
  profits are obtained by a perfect synergetic partnership, at the
  expense of the American citizen? Nowhere else on the face of
  the Earth is this a reality.

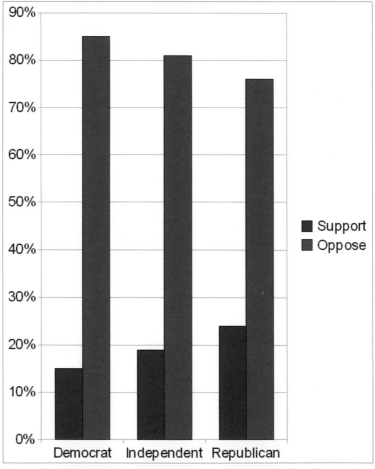

The public's views of the Citizens United v. Federal Election Commission
decision. CMBJ, 2010 Washington Post.

Citizen's United v. Federal Election Commission: In this landmark Supreme Court case, five Supreme Court justices voted that non-profit and for-profit corporations, labor unions, and other associations were to be treated as individual citizens to be granted the same First Amendment free speech privilege as US citizens. Granted, they are not allowed to contribute funds to political campaigns, but they are allowed to contribute to campaign advertising in order to influence voters for politicians who prescribe to their needs. Five Supreme Court justices actually considered corporations as citizens guaranteed the right of free speech under the First Amendment of the United States Constitution. Supreme Court justices are sworn to uphold the Constitution, which begins, "We the People . . ." President Obama called it "a major victory for big oil, Wall Street banks, health insurance companies, and the other powerful interests that marshal their power every day in Washington to drown out the voices of everyday Americans." Many of the middle and lower classes hardly have enough money to put food on the table, yet one of the three branches of their government made it legal for billion-dollar corporations to influence elected officials for the benefit of the corporation and their stockholders!

Colleges and universities: Once again, the United States is the only country in the world that saddles their college graduates with major financial burdens even before they begin their first job. In 2018, forty-four million Americans, approximately one out of every four adults, owe $1.5 trillion in student loan debt. Each of these student loans is roughly $37,000—$20,000 more than just thirteen years ago.[37] Just imagine starting your first real job—with rent, food, clothes, and other bills—when you are $37,000 in debt. How did this happen? For decades, American presidents and congressmen allowed universities to join the big business ranks. And what do businesses do? Well, for one, they compete with each other. So what did colleges begin doing? Branding and advertising to attract both students and professors, and because of student loans, the sky was the limit. What is also quite significant is that student loans, in general, don't affect the upper-income brackets because they tend to pay in cash, whereas

~much of the middle and lower classes must take out student loans—just one more wrinkle as to why the gap keeps growing between rich and poor.

It was effectively started on August 15, 1971, when over their morning coffee United States citizens (and the rest of the world) learned that the Bretton Woods Agreement of 1944—which set the standard that international currencies would all be backed by gold—was no longer in play. Nixon Shock, as it was termed, caused rumblings all over the world when he announced that US currency would no longer be dependent on gold. Not too many Americans knew it then, but that was one of the main precursors to the income inequality to come. The Fed, and other central banks around the world, could now place as much currency into circulation as it wanted, additional fiat money that through big business, real estate, and stock market investments and savings, all fed the wealthy to get richer, whereas the poor and middle class . . . well, the following sums it up: "After adjusting for inflation, however, today's average hourly wage has just about the same purchasing power as it did in 1978. . . ."[38]

"Income disparities have become so pronounced that America's top 10 percent now average more than nine times as much income as the bottom 90 percent."[39] Sixty-three percent of middle-class assets are tied up in their home; whereas the wealthy have three-quarters of their savings in investments.[40]

Then came the ingenious 401Ks that encouraged the working class to put their life savings into the stock market, effectively dissolving their pensions, leading the way for trillions of dollars of retirement money lost in the stock market debacles of 2001–2002, the 2008 financial crisis, and potentially a future one as well. Not only did it adversely affect American families across the nation, but it turned the big business of the stock market—Wall Street, investment firms, and the banks—into even greater financial business empires than they had been.

Then it was off to the races with the 1999 elimination of the Roosevelt-era Glass-Steagall Act, which helped tremendously to pave the way for the financial crisis just nine years later when Americans lost $12.8 trillion total[41] and 2.6 million jobs in the first year of the crisis.[42]

Suffice it to say that "We the People . . ." slowly but surely became "We the Big Business . . ." which led not surprisingly into "We the Wealthy," leaving millions of Americans by the wayside. According to a May 2018 study by the United Way ALICE project, 43 percent — more than four out of ten households in the United States—don't earn enough to be able to afford to eat properly, pay their rent, health-care, or own a cell phone.[43]

How Collusion Occurs

Government agencies have done a wonderful job through the years of making it seem as though any version of an incident other than the official story was a meaningless conspiracy theory. Some of what you'll learn in this volume will be predicated on conspiracy theories. One of the arguments against these theories is that it is impossible to hide such huge operations—that there are just too many people involved to keep them quiet. In actuality, conspiracies work not only because the general public wants to believe the official story, but also because each piece of evidence left behind when treated separately isn't compelling enough to pay that much attention to.

On November 24, 1963, the investigation into the assassination of President John F. Kennedy by Lee Harvey Oswald had just begun. Only one FBI officer and one Secret Service agent had barely enough time to get Oswald's name, let alone siphon all the information that he had to give. Less than forty-eight hours after Oswald's arrest, Jack Ruby, a nightclub owner with known ties to the mafia, broke into the Dallas jail and past police officers to shoot Oswald dead at point blank range, eliminating any chance of knowing who Oswald was, what his motives were, and the wealth of information he possessed.

On September 13, 2001, the FBI and CIA—probably the two largest clandestine domestic and international espionage agencies in the world that had supposedly bumbled their way into allowing such a horrendous act to occur on United States soil—uncovered all of the details of what occurred on September 11 in just forty-eight hours, including the names of all nineteen hijackers and details of the plan that originated from their leader, Osama Bin Laden. Suddenly, out of the clear blue, the American intelligence community developed thorough investigative prowess. It took Colonel Lafayette Baker, under instructions from Secretary of War Edwin Stanton, only forty-eight hours to discover every detail of the Abraham Lincoln assassination including all of the conspirators and their location. He almost conclusively knew the plot and the perpetrators prior to Lincoln's murder. Collusion was rife in 1865, and there's little doubt that it also played a part in the JFK assassination and the events of 9/11.

As has been pointed out, one of the very first arguments used to counter the efforts of proving that an incident has been caused by additional people is that it is too hard to create a cover-up—there are just too many operatives who could or would be whistleblowers and informants. There are dozens of people connected with the Kennedy assassination who died in mysterious and bizarre ways. A few deserve considerable attention.

Mary Pinchot Meyer was JFK's lover, and one of the close friends of both JFK and Jackie. In 1944, painter Mary Pinchot met Cord Meyer, a marine who was recuperating from shrapnel injuries, including the loss of an eye. They married a year later, subsequently had three sons, and eventually settled in Georgetown where Cord began working at the CIA in 1951 in the espionage and counterintelligence branch. Meyer was part of Operation Mockingbird, a CIA program to influence the media. Disillusioned with the CIA, Meyer quit in January 1954. At about this time, newlyweds Senator John F. Kennedy and Jackie moved in down the street from the Meyers, and the two couples became very good friends, especially Jackie and Mary who went on many walks together. In November, Cord returned to the CIA as head of the International Organizations Division, spending much time in Europe, and in 1958, Mary filed for divorce.

Moving very well within Georgetown's elite social circles, Mary was friendly with the *Washington Post*'s Ben Bradlee (who was also her

Mary Pinchot Meyer at JFK's 46th birthday Party on the presidential yacht Sequoia. Robert Knudsen, 1963.

brother-in-law), ABC News reporter Lisa Howard, chief of CIA Counterintelligence James Angleton and his wife, and Bobby and Ethel Kennedy, who moved into John and Jackie's home after the latter moved into the White House. In late 1961 or early 1962, President Kennedy and Mary began an affair, and she told friends that she was keeping a diary. She and JFK were presumably very much in love, and pacifist Mary quite possibly influenced the president's views on nuclear disarmament with Russia and rapprochement with Cuba. It was no secret that the FBI was keeping a file on her, and the CIA later admitted that they were bugging her phone.

Peter Janney, in his book *Mary's Mosaic: The CIA Conspiracy to Murder John F. Kennedy, Mary Pinchot Meyer, and Their Vision for World Peace*, details the results of his investigation into her 1964 death:

After Dallas, amid utter horror and shock, Mary had taken it upon herself to discover and make sense of the truth of the conspiracy that had taken place—only to realize the magnitude of the second conspiracy, a cover-up taking place right before her eyes. There, in her diary, she had reached an understanding. It was her own mosaic of people, events, circumstances, and exploration that informed her understanding—not only of the evil that had taken place in Dallas, but of the villainous darkness that was now enveloping all of America. She had furiously confronted her ex-husband, Cord Meyer, possibly Jim Angleton as well, with what she had discovered, not fully realizing the extent of their own diabolical ruthlessness. The Warren Report was ultimately nothing more than a house of cards; once ignited with the right matchstick, it would be engulfed in flames. If Mary courageously went public with who she was, and what she knew, making clear her position in the final years of Jack's life, people with influence would take notice; the fire of suspicion around Dallas would erupt into a conflagration. She had to be eliminated.[44]

Friend Timothy Leary claims that Mary called him the day after the assassination and said, "They couldn't control him anymore. He was changing too fast. He was learning too much . . . They'll cover everything up. I gotta come see you. I'm scared. I'm afraid. Be careful."[45]

Prior to her death, Meyer told friends that she believed that there had been some people in her house while she was away, and that she believed she saw someone leaving her apartment as she was entering. Both incidents were reported to the police. On October 12, 1964, less than a year after the assassination, Mary was shot at or near point-blank range in the head and heart while walking along the Chesapeake and Ohio towpath in Georgetown. A car mechanic, working on a car nearby, heard a woman shouting, and as he ran toward the scene claimed that he saw an African American male standing over her body. Police shortly arrived, catching Raymond Crump, who not only fit the description but also had his fly open.

The murder weapon was never found, and the mechanic couldn't positively identify Crump. Due to circumstantial evidence, Crump was not convicted. The murder remains an unsolved mystery. Six weeks prior to his death, author C. David Heymann asked Cord Meyers who he thought killed Mary. "The same sons of bitches," he hissed, "that killed John F. Kennedy."[46] Significantly, during the arrest and trial of Crump, it was never reported that the murdered woman had been JFK's mistress or that her ex-husband was a CIA operative. As a matter of fact, the presiding judge in a pretrial motion didn't even allow the private life of Mary to be mentioned during the trial.[47] Not surprisingly, the case was of very little interest to the public, exactly what a cover-up would strongly desire.

Mary Pinchot Myer's good friend Lisa Howard was fired by ABC News for her involvement in Kennedy's Castro negotiation dealings (to be discussed fully later in the chapter, "The Second Successful American Coup d'état: The JFK Assassination") and died on July 4, 1965. Found staggering in a parking lot, it was reported that she committed suicide by taking 100 phenobarbital pills because she was depressed over losing her job.

Columnist Dorothy Kilgallen, who was also a regular panelist on the television series *What's My Line?*, was deeply involved in the Kennedy assassination story and convinced that Oswald was innocent. She once wrote that if Marina Oswald told the "whole story of her life with President Kennedy's alleged assassin, it would split open the front pages of newspapers all over the world."[48] Kilgallen, the only person to interview Jack Ruby, was writing a book to be titled *Murder One* and bragged that she would reveal the contents of the interview and the real story behind the assassination. Kilgallen told friends that she was close to discovering who actually killed the president. Soon afterward, on November 8, 1965, Kilgallen was found dead, sitting upright in bed with a book on her lap, an apparent suicide by alcohol and barbiturates. Her personal hairdresser, Marc Sinclaire, who often woke Kilgallen, immediately concluded that she had been murdered:

- According to Sinclaire, Kilgallen would never have gone to bed dressed as she was discovered, with a blouse over her nightgown.
- She was in the master bedroom, which, according to Sinclaire, she hadn't occupied for many years.
- Kilgallen had Robert Ruark's novel *The Honey Badger* on her lap. Her reading glasses were nowhere to be found. Sinclaire pointed out that Dorothy could not read without eyeglasses and had already read the book several weeks earlier, having discussed it with Sinclaire.
- Although Kilgallen always removed her fake eyelashes and makeup prior to retiring each night, she was still wearing them when her body was found.

Though it is true that Kilgallen was in serious financial trouble and feared that she would be forced to sell her beloved Manhattan apartment, she was also expecting to earn a fortune from *Murder One*, making it highly unlikely that her death was a depression-caused suicide.

The kicker, however, is that longtime JFK mistress Florence Pritchett Smith, who was Kilgallen's close friend (both wrote for the same newspaper and appeared on *What's My Line?*), died just two days later. Even though Smith suffered from leukemia, it is just too much of a coincidence. Was Smith in possession of Kilgallen's missing notes, or did she just know too much?

The Kennedy assassination is a classic example of how cover-ups are covered up. H. R. Haldeman, President Nixon's chief of staff, claimed in his book *The Ends of Power* that: "After Kennedy was killed, the CIA launched a fantastic cover-up. The CIA literally erased any connection between Kennedy's assassination and the CIA . . . in fact, Counterintelligence Chief James Angleton of the CIA called Bill Sullivan of the FBI and rehearsed the questions and answers they would give to the Warren Commission investigators."[49]

American Money Powers Honed Its Skills from Historical Lessons Learned during Britain's Nineteenth Century Empire

While the United States was predominantly the number one power during most of the twentieth century, that achievement went to Great Britain for most of the nineteenth, with the possible turning point coming during the Spanish-American War. In just a few short months, the United States quickly exerted its influence with its defeat of Spain, ousting the European power from Cuba and Puerto Rico in Latin America, and the Philippines, Guam, and Hawaii in the Pacific. But in the 1800s, England reigned supreme. The Royal Navy was superior on the high seas, easily protecting the empire's exports of manufactured goods. This included Manchester's valuable textile industry, which, by the way, is one of the major reasons why the British discreetly backed the Confederate states against the North during the US Civil War. Britain wanted Southern cotton to flow directly to its textile mills, transported on its ships, rather than first going north to the Union, where it was subject to tariffs.

British bankers controlled international banking with loans for trade and railroad growth. And the more money they lent to foreign nations (at a huge profit, of course), the more the English infrastructure and British citizens suffered. In effect, bankers and industrialists had convinced Parliament to issue a statement that they supported absolute free trade, and several years later Parliament repealed the Corn Laws which had protected their agriculture industry, opening the way for cheap labor policies. The trading houses and bankers made a fortune while the workers suffered, creating a huge wealth gap, with the money powers controlling Parliament where the legislators did their dirty work. This unequal distribution of assets made wealth inequality almost identical to America's 150 years or so later.

Anti-Corn-Law League plaque on 69 Fleet Street, London EC4. Man vyi, 2008.

This was termed globalization in the 1900s, with American businesses by the droves going to Mexico, China, Taiwan, and any other place where they could usurp the American worker for cheaper wages, manufacture a cheaper product, and then import that same product for sale to the worker who is now out of a job and has no income. And in addition, paying zero federal taxes since their manufacturing plant is out of the country. Nineteenth-century British free trade was given a whole new outlook and lease on life, especially due to all the free trade treaties between the industrialized countries around the world. Enter Donald Trump.

A Tufts University study showed that during the 1950s and 1960s, roughly 25 percent of American workers were employed in the manufacturing sector, yet roughly forty-five years later, in 2004, that number dwindled to 11 percent![50] Apple products come in a box marked, "Designed by Apple in California. Assembled in (name the foreign country)."[51]

As in nineteenth-century England, late twentieth and twenty-first-century America saw the elite skyrocket in wealth and power from basically the same policies. Capitalism, a brilliant form of free enterprise isn't to blame, nor is democracy—that form of government enables human beings to live free and to govern themselves. The problem at the core is the multitudes of the representatives of the people throughout the centuries who allowed the elite in powerhouse countries as England and the United States to gain the upper hand, controlling the wealth and power over the same people who voted those legislators into office in the first place to protect their interests.

Part Two:

The Timeline

A photographic reproduction of John Trumbull's 1819 painting of the presentation to Congress of the Declaration of Independence. The original hangs in the Capitol rotunda. John Trumbull, 1819.

A graphic of the US Constitution with a flag background. US Airforce Graphic, 2012.

1832: The Demise of the Second Bank of the United States

An 1833 lithograph by Edward W. Clay, published by H. R. Robinson, N.Y.

This lithograph by Edward W. Clay praises Andrew Jackson for destroying the Second Bank of the United States with his "Removal Notice" (i.e., removal of federal deposits). Nicolas Biddle is portrayed as the Devil, along with several speculators and hirelings, flee as the bank collapses while Jackson's supporters cheer. Edward W. Clay (Unknown date 1832).

Jacksonian Democracy, aptly named for its founder President Andrew Jackson, is as some scholars have claimed a contradiction of terms. It was an authentic democratic movement, yet dedicated itself mainly to the white man. To the Jacksonian Democrat, democracy meant equal rights and limited government to ensure that the upper class did not enrich itself further by taking control of public institutions. They strived to rid government of the wealthy and unelected private bankers who were attempting to dominate the country's economy.

This era saw the first well-organized political parties, and opposing the Jacksonian Democrats were the Whigs, who would later become the Radical Republican faction of the Republican Party. The Whigs saw themselves as highly nationalistic, pro-banker, pro-business and pro-corporation, and anti-states' rights, yet what really brought them together was their opposition to President Jackson's veto of the extension of the Second Bank of the United States.

In 1791, the Bank of the United States was formed with a twenty-year charter by Congress to handle federal funds, establish a national currency, and to be the fiscal agent for the country. *Two-thirds of the bank stock was held by British interests.*[52] Due to a lack of support, in large part because of the foreign stock ownership, the bank's charter was not renewed in 1811, putting the bank out of business. The War of 1812 brought about financial difficulty to the country, and by 1816, America was ready for another foray into central banking. The Second Bank of the United States was then ratified with another twenty-year charter, with very similar functions to the First Bank.

President Jackson believed the bank should be abolished, and proceeded to veto Congress's extension bill, feeling that the bank contained too many negatives for the American people:

- The wealthy simply would become wealthier.
- A few families would control the people's money.
- Bankers would have more control over members of the legislature.
- It would be too easy for foreign interests (British bankers) to exert their influence over the government.

- The nation's financial strength would be concentrated in a single institution,
- Northern industrialists would have more power over western and southern states.

And, Jackson and many congressmen felt that this central bank was unconstitutional. Article One, Section Eight, Clause Five of the US Constitution states, "Congress shall have power to coin Money, regulate the Value thereof, and of foreign Coin, and fix the Standard of Weights and Measures." When the Second Bank of the United States bill got to his desk, President Jackson vetoed it, saying in part:

> A bank of the United States is in many respects convenient for the Government and for the people. Entertaining this opinion, and deeply impressed with the belief that some of the powers and privileges possessed by the existing bank are unauthorized by the Constitution, subversive of the rights of the States, and dangerous to the liberties of the people, I felt it my duty . . . to call to the attention of Congress to the practicability of organizing an institution combining its advantages and obviating these objections. I sincerely regret that in the act before me I can perceive none of those modifications of the bank charter which are necessary, in my opinion, to make it compatible with justice, with sound policy, or with the Constitution of our country.[53]

Timeline to the first assassination attempt on a US president:

- 1833: With the Second Bank scheduled to be dissolved in 1836, President Jackson withdraws all federal funds from this private bank.
- January 8, 1835: President Jackson completely pays off the US national debt. For the first and only time in its history, the country does not owe a single penny to the private bankers running America's central bank. Jackson thus becomes the first president, prior to Lincoln and Garfield, to exert his total independence from the money powers.

An etching illustrating an attempted assassination of President Andrew Jackson by Richard Lawrence on January 30, 1835, in Washington, DC, drawn from a sketch by an eyewitness. George Endicott, lithographer and publisher, New York, 1835.

- January 30, 1835: Just twenty-two days after exerting this independence, President Jackson is leaving a funeral when a so-called deranged man named Richard Lawrence springs from behind a pillar and fires twice from two single-shot pistols from thirteen and three feet respectively. Luckily both guns misfire, most likely due to the moisture in the air.

Senator George Poindexter and his close friend Senator Henry Clay were both Whigs, the political party that vigorously opposed Jackson's administration. Although Poindexter was elected in 1830 as a Jacksonian Democrat, by the time he left office he was totally anti-Jackson and pro-central banking. What you won't read in your children's history books is that Richard Lawrence, the would-be assassin, was a house painter who just happened to have painted Poindexter's house just a few months prior to the assassination attempt. What a coincidence. Poindexter's Mississippi constituency apparently believed his involvement in the conspiracy, because he was later voted out of office.[54]

So, if Lawrence had been successful in ridding America of its president, the Second Bank of the United States most likely would have been extended for at least another twenty years, and the bankers would have continued to profit enormously from the US economy. They tried and failed. Unfortunately, their aim got a lot better in the years to come.

You will soon learn that a good portion of the evidence points to the Radical Republicans, successors to the Whigs and somewhat driven by the money powers as well, as being directly responsible for John Wilkes Booth's assassination of President Abraham Lincoln.

Manifest Destiny: Domestic Imperialism

John Gast's 1872 painting "American Progress" depicts Manifest Destiny—how God in the form of the angel brought settlers from the light of the technological East (notice the railroad and telegraph) into the darkness of the West (the genocide of the American Indian and buffalo). Autry National Center, 1872.

In 1845 influential newspaper editor John L. O'Sullivan coined the phrase which became the idea that shaped American history: "Manifest Destiny." In order to conceptualize America's thirst for expansion, O'Sullivan explained it as follows:

> . . . the right of our manifest destiny to overspread and to possess the whole of the continent which Providence has given us for the development of the great experiment of liberty and federative development of self-government entrusted to us. It is right such as that of the tree to the space of air and the earth suitable for the full expansion of its principle and destiny of growth.[55]

Broken down into its literal components, one can easily see what O'Sullivan intended:

"Manifest": To prove.

"Destiny": The inevitable or necessary fate to which a particular person or thing is destined; one's lot. A predetermined course of events considered as something beyond human power or control.

Financial monopoly: Increased profits achievable only through expansion—has been accomplished for centuries by nations and their dictators, aptly creating empires for themselves. But the economic elite in the United States and their financial allies in Britain had a huge stumbling block in the United States—*democracy*—where the people, not a dictator, controlled the actions of the military and the goals of the government through its elected officials. So, for virtually the very first time in history, the citizenry had to be convinced that American imperialism was in each citizen's best interests. And for the first time, but far from the last, the country invoked God to do the dirty work.

The United States began a campaign of Manifest Destiny, brainwashing the electorate on the notion that it was America's natural and God-given right to expand its borders from ocean to ocean, giving the military and the government the right to claim land on their behalf, and to conduct a genocide of the American Indian who had claimed the land as theirs for centuries.

Not only did Congress have a hand in this, but possibly for the first time, the president of the United States, as can be seen in President James Knox Polk's 1845 inaugural address:

> Foreign powers do not seem to appreciate the true character of our Government. Our Union is a confederation of independent States, whose policy is peace with each other and all the world. *To enlarge its limits is to extend the dominions of peace over additional territories* and increasing millions. The world has nothing to fear from military ambition in our Government. . . . Foreign powers should therefore look on the annexation of Texas to the United States not as the conquest of a nation seeking to extend her dominions by arms and violence, but as the peaceful acquisition of a territory once her own, by adding another member to our confederation, with the consent of that member, thereby diminishing the chances of war *and opening to them new and ever-increasing markets for their products.*[56] [Italics inserted by S. H. to add emphasis.]

In the period of Polk's inauguration speech and O'Sullivan's coining of the term "Manifest Destiny," the United States increased its borders by 60 percent—1.2 million square miles. From the 1840s to 1860s, the United States employed the notion that it was its *natural and God-given* right to expand its borders from ocean to ocean. It was for this reason that the Mexican-American War was fought from 1846–1848 to obtain Texas, and the purpose of stretching our borders across the continent to California, even giving some the thought that we should continue north into Canada.

In the year 1800 there were approximately six hundred thousand American Indians; by 1890, two hundred fifty thousand remained. In addition, nineteen thousand American men, women, and children died during the forty-plus years of the American Indian Wars, making it possible for the Vanderbilts, Rockefellers, Carnegies, and the other robber barons to make their fortunes by supplying a whole new breed of people—Western settlers and their families—with goods and services. And let's not forget the bankers J. P. Morgan, Kuhn Loeb, and a host of other financiers who invested heavily in western expansion.

An 1899 chromolithograph of US cavalry pursuing American Indians, artist unknown. Werner Company, Akron Ohio, Circa 1899.

They all came out of the 1800s with stuffed coffers beyond imagination, and were destined and ready to carry this financial fervor of expansion out into the Pacific Ocean and the Caribbean and South.

Manifest Destiny was also an indirect reason that the country became divided, culminating in the South seceding from the Union, forcing a Civil War where over a half million of our countrymen died. With each new territory came the same question: should it become a free state or a slave state, with violence and animosities heated beyond repair, until the attack by the South on Fort Sumter began the horrific War.

This expansionist agenda did not have bipartisan support and was, in fact, a collection of special interest groups that had different objectives and concerns. Nevertheless, due to the technological innovations of the transcontinental railroad, steamboats, and the telegraph ushering in modern long-distance communication, America now had the technological know-how to stretch its borders from ocean to ocean.

In the case of the American Indian, proponents of Manifest Destiny rationalized that pushing them further to the west was in their best interests since they no longer fit in the East. It was their salvation. The hypocrisy involved was that many of these Indians were quite sophisticated and civilized. The literacy rate of the Cherokee nation was higher than the white South up to the time of the Civil War. But the Cherokees were moved westward, so their land could be open for American expansion. And many of the farming Southeast tribes were moved to Oklahoma; trilingual, entrepreneurial Native Americans active in trade from Indiana, Illinois, and Michigan were forced out to the plains of Kansas, and so on until White America occupied most of their land.

On the fourth Thursday of each November, Americans eat turkey in grand family gatherings first celebrated in early colonial times in New England. Following their first harvested crop, colonists in Plymouth, led by then-Governor William Bradford, began a celebration of thanks to the Native Americans for teaching them how to survive in their new world. They apparently taught us extremely well. Two centuries later, the white man's Manifest Destiny proceeded to eat up the Indians, giving them no alternative but to fight, and rallying the American people with slogans portraying them as "savages," "scalpers," and "redskins."

It didn't take long for the money powers and industrialists to see what was before them as soon as Lewis and Clark made their findings known. The inventions of the steamboat, the railroads, and the telegraph made it all technologically feasible. The slogan of Manifest Destiny made the slaughter of a few hundred thousand men, women, and children—and the stealing of their land—legal. It enabled the settlers and the soldiers to follow God and the flag through the wilderness into the towns sprouting up around them, the scooping up of natural resources while money flowed into newly created town banks, the creation of a whole new labor force and retail outlets for the bankers, the railroad magnates, and the industrialists to begin to realize their fortunes. So what if several hundred thousand red people were in their way?

The year 1830 saw the passage of the Indian Removal Act, a move primarily designed to cleanse the Southern and west of the Mississippi lands for habitation by the immigrants swarming into the country.

In 1838, President Jackson's administration rounded up thirteen thousand Cherokees for relocation. Indians who had lived on their land for hundreds of years were being relocated one thousand miles away. Approximately four thousand of them perished along the way, victims of murder, starvation, and sickness, in what could only be termed a death march. It is just one instance of the genocide of the American Indian, and what the economic elite now choose to call the "casualties of war."

That same year, Indiana Governor David Wallace ordered the forced migration of more than 850 Potawatomi Indians to Kansas, 660 miles away. The two-month trek cost the lives of forty-two of the Indians, many dying most likely from typhoid fever. They marched daily from eight in the morning to four in the afternoon and received their only meal of the day when they stopped for the night.

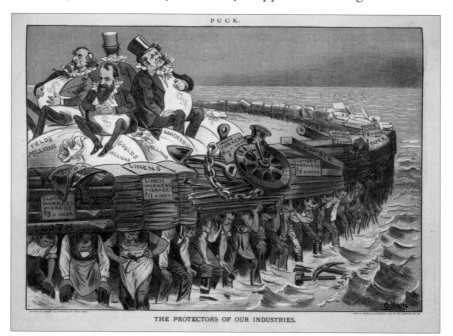

Cartoon showing Cyrus Field, Jay Gould, Cornelius Vanderbilt, and Russell Sage, seated on bags of "millions" on a large raft, and being carried by workers of various professions. *Puck* magazine, Mayer Merkel & Ottmann lith., N.Y.; Published by Keppler & Schwarzmann, 1883.

This economic expansion for the benefit of a few was not an isolated event. The only way the United States could have evolved from thirteen colonies into three thousand miles of forty-eight continental unified states in a relatively few short years was by a highly structured, well-oiled team consisting of members of the House and Senate to get the necessary laws passed through Congress, the justices to make those laws legal when needed, the media to rally American citizens around God and the flag (or, in this particular instance, Manifest Destiny), the military to carry out the dirty work, and some presidents in their hip pocket.

The robber barons were essentially the first millionaires, in the right place at the right time, making their fortunes from these new markets earned through Manifest Destiny. The early American elite learned so much, and then spread that knowledge so efficiently to future generations.

April 12, 1861: The Confederate Attack on Fort Sumter, Effectively Beginning the Worst Conflict in American History

Photographic reproduction of a work of art depicting the 1864 Battle of Cold Harbor, in which thousands of American lives were lost. Kurz and Allison, 1888.

Although the result of the Civil War was the elimination in the United States of one of the greatest horrors of mankind, slavery was neither the immediate cause of the war nor was it even why it was fought. Americans have, to a large degree, been misinformed and miseducated into believing that the Civil War was fought as a moral crusade against slavery.

Abraham Lincoln personally abhorred the institution of slavery but could see no solution to the problem. His sole purpose in fighting the Civil War was to *preserve the Union* at all cost, not to free the slaves. Even the famous Emancipation Proclamation that freed all slaves in rebellion states (but not the border states—including Delaware, Kentucky, Maryland, and Missouri—where slavery was still legal) was a calculated move on his part to prevent the British from entering the war on the side of the Confederacy. The British people would never put up with their government siding with slavery.

When the Confederates attacked Fort Sumter, the rallying cry of the North was not "Free the slaves." Rather, it was "Preserve the Union." Slavery was most certainly an issue leading up to the Civil War, with the vocal and activist abolitionists leading the way, but it was not of concern to most northerners. Many Unionists couldn't care less, with some even favoring slavery, since it benefited their economic position. Without slavery, Southern cotton would have been more expensive to cultivate and harvest, and without the northern textile industry which depended so heavily on Southern cotton, Union workers would lose their jobs and the economy would suffer. Furthermore, only four states in the North even allowed free blacks to vote!

Eli Whitney's invention of the cotton gin, combined with free slave labor, made the cultivation of cotton a highly profitable industry for the southern plantations. The slave unfortunately became an integral part in not only the southern economy but the northern states and European economies as well via cotton exports. The first half of the nineteenth century saw the country split into two very different regions along implicit social, economic, and political lines. By the 1850s, the rift was almost too deep to fix. In 1860, the South's cotton represented a whopping 57 percent of US exports. The highly industrialized North needed cheap labor to work their factories, making the

African American slaves using the First cotton gin, 1790-1800, drawn by William L. Sheppard. Illustration in *Harper's Weekly*, 1869 Dec. 18, p. 813. *Harpers Weekly's* illustration depicting event of some seventy years earlier. The illustration is of a Roller Cotton Gin and not an illustration of a Whitney Spike Gin or Holmes Saw Gin.

United States a prime destination for European immigrants who not only manned the factories, but also built the railroads in the North and settled in the West. There was very little in the South to entice them.

The South, meanwhile, resisted any temptation to industrialize. As a result, almost all manufactured items were imported from the northern industrialized states and Europe. The North, in order to protect their industries from cheap foreign competition, began instituting protective tariffs, or taxes, on all imports. These tariffs, which caused consumers in the South to pay more for their goods, became the federal government's major source of income.

The first southern tax rebellion came in 1832 when South Carolina passed the Ordinance of Nullification, which refused to collect the tariffs and threatened secession. President Jackson sent federal troops to Charleston, and a crisis was avoided, but the lines were set.

As the century wore on, western states such as Ohio, Indiana, and

Michigan aligned themselves with the North. These states depended on internal improvements for survival and desperately needed the money that the Union acquired from their tariffs. Whereas half the population of the United States lived in the South in 1800, by 1850 only a third lived there. Through compromise after compromise, states that were added to the country became either free or slave states, but the South found its representation dwindling in the House of Representatives due to the high number of European immigrants arriving in the North. Southerners were losing their voice in the government and were fearful of their very existence. They felt they were being backed into a corner, with secession and the formation of a new country their only way out.

The South was not rebelling or even instigating a rebellion. Thirteen states decided to go their own way, which is what the original thirteen colonies did when they seceded from Great Britain. And, ironically, it was primarily for the same basic reason—high taxation.[57] The US Constitution does not only prohibit secession, but it can be interpreted as enabling it in the Ninth Amendment and Tenth Amendment by stating that the states/citizens will be the guardians of their own liberty.

Charles Dickens noted at the time that it was purely a fiscal matter. The North could not let the South go peacefully, because the loss of the South posed a potential economic threat from losing revenue from the tariffs. There was no federal income tax. Most revenue coming into the country was from the tariffs imposed on imports arriving at southern ports. To make matters even worse, the bulk of that revenue went to the northern infrastructure.[58] The *New York Evening Post* editorialized on this point on March 12, 1861:

> That either the revenue from duties must be collected in the ports of the rebel states, or the ports must be closed to importations from abroad, it is generally admitted. If neither of these things be done, our revenue laws are substantially repealed; the sources which supply our treasury will be dried up; we shall have no money to carry on the government; the nation will become bankrupt before the next crop of corn is ripe.[59]

Taxes on southern imports accounted for approximately 83 percent of the Union's revenues.[60] Without the Union tariffs, southerners would begin to purchase European goods at much lower prices, which would be a huge blow to the northern economy, and southern states would begin to control their own ports and duties, inducing the railroads and other buyers to use southern ports rather than those in the north. The North would then have to reduce its tariffs, effectively reducing their revenues, with the possible result being economic ruin. Northern industrialists realized that they would be competing against a South engaging in free trade. Not only would tax revenue decline, but trade as well.

No, it wasn't slavery at all, but the power of money that forced President Abraham Lincoln to go to war. Six hundred thousand US citizens died, another million were maimed. Fifty thousand southern civilians were killed, and cities and property destroyed. All due to the prospect of almost certain northern economic death.

1865: The Attempted Coup d'état of the United States of America

The North could never let the South go peacefully. Without those protective tariffs, the North would most likely not survive. Its sphere of influence over the southern states would be lost forever and, in the unlikely event that the South was victorious, those same men would survive. The South would require bankers and industry. In addition, once victory was attained, they would mold their southern neighbors into an economic structure that would not only suit their needs, but one that they could profit from beyond imagination. This would be known as Southern Reconstruction. Their political allies were the Radical Republicans who split the country with their anti-slavery stance. With the war now won, there was only one man standing in the way of unimaginable profits—President Abraham Lincoln. They had failed with Andrew Jackson, and they weren't about to make the same mistake.

April 14, 1865: The official story has been rattled about for more than a century and a half. John Wilkes Booth hated Lincoln due mainly to his ties with the issue of slavery. After

ABRAHAM LINCOLN,

Abraham Lincoln, assassinated April 14, 1865, Popular Graphic Arts.

Lucy Lambert Hale (1842–1915), the daughter of John P. Hale. Matthew Brady, 1863.

the failure of an oil-drilling business in Pennsylvania in which he had invested $6,000 with two other fellow actors, Booth traveled to Montreal where he allegedly met with members of the Confederacy. By this time, the Union had the upper hand in the war between the states, and presumably as a last-ditch effort, the Confederacy enlisted Booth to kidnap the president, holding him in exchange for the release of tens of thousands of Confederate prisoners of war. The South hoped that they could use these freed soldiers to mount an offensive.

Booth then settled in Washington, DC, and proceeded to piece together the plan, allegedly aided by Mary Surrat, Lewis Payne, David Herold, George Atzerodt, and a host of other minor figures. Nestling himself quite cozily into Washington's upper class social and political circles, Booth finally became engaged in late 1864 or early 1865 to Lucy Hale, the daughter of Senator John Hale, the abolitionist Radical Republican from New Hampshire. The Hales resided in the National Hotel, the same establishment that housed John Booth.

Learning that the president was to attend a play on March 17 at the Campbell Hospital outside of Washington, the conspirators prepared to kidnap Lincoln from his carriage along the route. However, the president decided instead to deliver a speech at the 140th Indiana Regiment. The long-awaited plan had gone awry. And as far as Booth was concerned, death was now in store for President Lincoln.

On the morning of April 14, Booth became aware that the president would attend a Ford's Theatre performance that evening. General Lee had already surrendered at Appomattox, the war was over, but that didn't stop John Wilkes Booth. Rounding up his cohorts, he assigned Atzerodt to kill Vice President Andrew Johnson. Paine was to murder Secretary of State William Seward who was bedridden from

Ford's Theater in Washington, DC—Site of the assassination of President Abraham Lincoln. Matthew Brady, 1865.

a previous carriage accident, and Booth would take care of Lincoln. After being seen talking with Lucy in the National Hotel lobby that morning, Booth visited the theater to lay out his plan. As a successful actor who had played Ford's Theatre many times, Booth was not only familiar with the layout but also friendly with many of the employees and fellow actors, having free rein to move about at will. Later he rented a fast horse he would pick up at four in the afternoon. He then traveled to the hotel where Vice President Johnson resided, leaving a handwritten message for him, and returned to the National Hotel to await the evening's events.

After picking up his horse, Booth got to the theater with plenty of time to spare. He knew the play perfectly and the precise time when there would be a tremendous amount of laughter. At that moment, Booth took the stairs up to the presidential box, sprang in with a dagger and a derringer, shot President Lincoln in the head, and stabbed Major Henry Rathbone, who sat next to the president. Booth then jumped over the railing onto the stage, shouting, "*Sic semper tyrannis!*" ("Thus always to tyrants!") A flagpole got in the way of Booth's fall, causing him to break the fibula in his right leg. He ran out the back door to his horse and rode away in a frenzy.

Left: Washington, DC. President Lincoln's box at Ford's Theater. Civil War Glass Negatives, Library of Congress, 1865.

Right: Depiction of John Wilkes Booth leaning forward to shoot President Abraham Lincoln as he watches *Our American Cousin* at Ford's Theater in Washington, DC, on April 14, 1865. Unattributed; based on the depiction from a mechanical glass slide by T. M. McAllister of New York, 1865-75, circa 1900.

Lewis Payne had managed to stab Secretary of State Seward in the neck, wounding several others in Seward's house before escaping. George Atzerodt never perpetrated the planned attack on Vice President Johnson. Twelve days later, twenty-six mounted soldiers of the Sixteenth New York Cavalry caught up with Booth and David Herold, cornering them in a tobacco barn on a Virginia farm. Hoping to draw Booth out, the soldiers set fire to the structure. Booth may have given himself up, except for the fact that one of the soldiers, Boston Corbett, opened fire with a Colt revolver from the distance of a few yards through a large crack in the wall. Booth was removed from the barn, paralyzed, and suffered terrible pain for several hours. He finally asked for his hands to be

Boston Corbett sitting in a Gothic chair. Unattributed 1865.

raised to his face and died while uttering his last words, "Useless . . . useless" or, possibly, "Lucy, Lucy."

A religious fanatic, Corbett explained his actions with the remark, "God Almighty directed me," yet he officially stated afterward that he shot because he thought Booth was going to begin an attack. Corbett was placed under technical arrest, but the charges were dropped by Secretary of War Edwin Stanton. "The rebel is dead. The patriot lives," stated Stanton, and Corbett received his share of the reward money, which totaled $1,653.85 (approximately $25,000 in today's purchasing power).

The principals involved were found guilty by court martial, sentenced to death, and executed by hanging the very next day. The others were found guilty of lesser crimes and sentenced to various terms of imprisonment.

Mary Surratt, Lewis Powell, David Herold, and George Atzerodt, conspirators of Abraham Lincoln's assassination, on July 7, 1865, at Fort McNair in Washington, DC. Alexander Gardner, July 7, 1865.

Was Booth simply a Confederate sympathizer who hated Lincoln and the North so much that he wanted both the president and his upper echelon killed to throw the country into turmoil? Was political motivation his concern? All the evidence submitted at the trial shows quite clearly that there had been a plot against Lincoln in which many participants were involved, and that this plan had been in the works for months. There's no doubt about it. The only doubt and questions are why, and who financed it.

Abraham Lincoln was another potential threat to the powers that President Andrew Jackson so feared. Reelected, soon to be released from all the problems incurred during the Civil War, Lincoln understood that he was the only statesman in the world with the power and the will to see to it that the bankers did not control the government.

President Lincoln's quandary in 1862 when the Civil War was draining the Union financially was to print high-interest bank notes borrowed from the money powers or print interest-free government-issued greenbacks. Presumably with Col. Edmund Taylor's advice, the president's Legal Tender Act of 1862 was passed, issuing $150 million worth of "greenbacks" (paper money printed in bold green), and by 1863 there was just a little under $450 million worth of greenbacks in circulation. "[These greenbacks] served as legal tender for all debts, public and private, and were used to finance the Union's Civil War efforts."[61]

The money interests, though, were not going to be left out. Undoubtedly using their influence, Congress passed the National Bank Act of 1863, "from which point forward, all money in circulation would be created out of debt from bankers buying US government bonds in exchange for bank notes. By 1865, the national banks had 83 percent of all bank assets in the United States."[62] And the government paid a substantial amount of interest on those bonds that they sold to the money people.

Lincoln's greenback excursion was unheard of at the time. As a matter of fact, it was something that hadn't been done since the pre–American Revolution, when the colonists issued them with enormous success until King George put an end to it under pressure from the Bank of England. Well, things were no different in Lincoln's day.

Printing interest-free money was a dangerous thing to do. Lincoln's Civil War success made him an extremely popular president whose mandate could conceivably have caused him to continue printing interest-free money, and seeking to discontinue the National Bank Act just as President Jackson did with the Second Bank of the United States.

"Lincoln was assassinated by John Wilkes Booth on April 14, 1865; just five days after Lee surrendered to Grant. On April 12, 1866, Congress passed the Contraction Act which called for retiring Lincoln's greenbacks from circulation as soon as they came back to the Treasury in payment of taxes."[63]

It took just one year after his death to finalize the destruction of Lincoln's greenbacks. The private sector—the bankers throughout the world who had a vested interest in the American monetary system—could have been wiped out if Lincoln's national currency system was successful. Other countries would undoubtedly have followed suit, leading the way to a debt-free society, one in which the bankers of the world would become just another business. The Federal Reserve didn't yet exist, and there was no central bank, but the bankers in 1865 still held a monopoly on America's money and credit. Though President Jackson survived an assassination attempt following his successful war against the money interests, Lincoln was not as fortunate. But then again, Lincoln went one step further than Jackson—he created a national currency.

But there was another group on the political scene in the 1860s that desperately needed President Lincoln removed from office—the Radical Republicans. Following the election of 1860, these Radicals became a powerful force within Congress, favoring not only the abolition of slavery but total equality of blacks with fellow white citizens. Understand that this was *not* a social and moral ideal for which they strived. Though many such as Charles Sumner truly believed that slavery was evil, their ideology was to redo the South to resemble the North. Prominent members included Secretary of War Edwin Stanton, the Honorable Henry Wilson, John P. Hale, and the already-mentioned Sumner.

Lincoln's Reconstruction plan was assailed by the Radical

Secretary of War Edwin Stanton. E. &
H.T. Anthony (Firm), publisher, 1862.

Republicans who demanded that the power structure of the white South be removed. They felt that Lincoln was going to be far too charitable, having said in his second inaugural address, "With malice toward none. With charity toward all." Lincoln argued in his 1863 Proclamation of Amnesty and Reconstruction that the Southern states never even seceded, and that all southerners had to do was to sign a very simple loyalty oath to be readmitted to the Union. Radical Republicans in Congress then responded with the passage of the Wade-Davis Act, which said that 50 percent (not Lincoln's 10 percent) of eligible voters must sign the loyalty oath, and that provisional governors would be assigned to each southern state. Wade-Davis showed just how divided the presidency and Congress were. Lincoln wanted to ease the Confederacy back into the Union; the Radicals demanded to bring them to their knees.

Lincoln vetoed the bill, effectively killing it, but the damage had been done, though in Lincoln's case it spurred him on to a landslide second-term victory. With Lincoln as president through 1868, the bankers, financiers, and the Radical Republicans would almost never have accomplished their goals. The only way was for another administration to take power.

The official story is that Booth wanted Lincoln, Johnson, and Seward out of the way in order to throw the country into turmoil as retribution for the victory over the South. On the contrary, the author claims that Booth was paid to pave the way for another administration to prevent Lincoln's production of debt-free money and to enable the Radical Republicans to proceed with their Southern Reconstruction plans. In other words, a *non-military, peaceful coup d'état.*

Booth had allegedly been paid handsomely in gold by Confederate sympathizers in Montreal to kidnap the president for the ransom of tens of thousands of Confederate soldiers. When his kidnap plan went awry on March 17, the war was still raging, with almost another month to go prior to Lee's surrender at Appomattox. Though his personal sentiments aligned itself with the plot, this was not a personal vendetta but a business arrangement. Unless he was paid to change the plan, Booth would have found another ransom alternative.

In 1865, the statute of succession when both the president and vice president were no longer able to perform their duties was for the senate president pro tempore to assume the duties of the presidency.[64] That man, who had been elected on March 7, 1865, just a few weeks prior to Lincoln's death, was Republican Lafayette S. Foster. He was once a Whig, the central forerunner political party to the Radicals.

In effect, if George Atzerodt and Lewis Payne had succeeded in killing Vice President Johnson and Secretary of State Seward, the election of 1864 would have effectively been rendered null and void. Radical Republican Secretary of War Edwin Stanton, without the moderate Republican Seward's opposition, would have completely controlled the cabinet regarding the Southern Reconstruction. As for the two survivors, Johnson was impeached in an attempt to end his presidency, and Seward continued to serve Johnson as Secretary of State, even using all of his power behind the scenes to prevent Johnson's removal from office. Had the impeachment proved successful, Seward would almost certainly have been replaced by the newly appointed president. The April 15, 1865 attempted coup d'état would have finally come to fruition.

The why has been proposed; the next question is *how*.

There is no doubt that John Wilkes Booth was a megalomaniac whose total sympathies were with the Confederacy, and he hated Lincoln, not so much for his desire to preserve the Union but due to his anti-slavery stance. But there's also no doubt that Booth ran in circles where only the privileged were allowed entry. He mingled with many of the most influential politicians and financiers in the country and was well-known in those circles. A ladies' man who was never without a woman, they seemed unable to turn him down, many commenting that his eyes made him irresistible. Such a man derives a certain power from this, and it's very difficult to believe that he was willing to leave such a way of life. To the contrary, it's easy for one to believe that he was eager for it to continue. And this privileged way of life requires money—lots of it. Paine was a Confederate deserter. Was he to do it for free and for the cause of the Confederacy? Was Booth really going to kill Lincoln, make his way back to the South, and live in the ruins of southern reconstruction?

The war was over, Confederate soldiers could keep their weapons and their horses, and Lincoln was calling for the rebel states to come back into the fold. Knowing intimately many of the political figures that he was socializing with, Booth had to know that killing Lincoln out of hatred was not only futile but totally against the Southern cause and his own ambitions. Megalomaniac, yes. Stupid, no.

Booth had a brilliant plan, which also included his escape route. If it weren't for the fact that he unexpectedly broke his leg, there's a good possibility he would have never been caught. As far as he was concerned, he was probably going to be a free man somewhere around the world who would need plenty of the greenbacks. But who would be willing and able to supply that much money for him and his co-conspirators? There's only one group of people who had both the motive and the wherewithal to have supplied Booth and company with enough cash to make it worth their while—the Northern money interests and their cohorts, a splinter group of the Radical Republicans.

Lincoln appointed Edwin Stanton secretary of war in 1862, and he promptly became highly critical of the government. When Supreme Court Chief Justice Roger B. Taney died in 1864, Stanton petitioned Lincoln to be his replacement but was turned down. Stanton's wish would not be fulfilled until four years later, when President Ulysses S. Grant appointed him to the nation's highest court and the Senate confirmed him on the same day. As war secretary, Stanton hired Lafayette Baker to head the National Detective Police (NDP), in charge of Union Counterintelligence. It was Baker who was called upon by Stanton immediately upon Lincoln's assassination to apprehend the culprits.

. . . Lincoln had died and Edwin Stanton had taken over the government, declaring martial law. What he wanted more than anything at that moment was John Wilkes Booth, offering $100,000 for his dead-or-alive capture, preferably dead. Before Lincoln had been shot, Baker embarrassingly admitted later, he and Stanton had no knowledge of the conspiracy. Yet, within two days, all of the conspirators were in custody. Somehow, Baker knew exactly where he could find the alcoholic George A. Atzerodt whose nerve had failed him when it came time to kill Vice President Andrew Johnson. Somehow, he knew that Seward's would-be assassin, Lewis Payne, could be found in the Washington, DC, boarding house of Mary Surratt, hiding under a bed in a third-floor room.

Mary Surratt's boarding house; meeting place of Lincoln conspirators. Mathew Brady and Levin Corbin Handy, Between 1890 and 1910.

Somehow, the illustrious Colonel Baker knew to arrest Edward Spangler, the carpenter at Ford's Theater who had made a portable barrier for Booth so he could successfully bar the inside of the door that led to Lincoln's box once the assassin had entered this restricted but unguarded hallway. Somehow, Baker's keen but unexplained perceptions deduced that Spangler had also drilled a hole in the door leading to Lincoln's box so Booth, while standing in the outer hallway could peer into it unmolested and know when the president was most vulnerable.[65]

The very man who was responsible for protecting the life of the president had, twenty-four hours before the assassination, no idea of the identities of the conspirators. But then suddenly, inexplicably, almost magically, Lafayette Baker possessed all the answers within forty-eight hours, including the exact obscure escape route taken by John Wilkes Booth and David Herold. . . .[66]

Following his firing by President Johnson, Baker published a book announcing that he gave Booth's diary to Stanton immediately following the assassin's capture. Forced by Congress, Stanton finally produced the diary, but with eighteen missing pages that have never been found—eighteen pages that potentially and presumably implicate Stanton and the others in the conspiracy.

Around the time that the assassination plan began to materialize, Booth began his triumphant starring engagement at the Boston Museum in the longest appearance of his career as a star, from April 25 to May 28, 1864. An actress who performed with Booth remembered that "the stage door was always blocked with silly women waiting to catch a glimpse, as he passed, of his superb face and figure."[67]

It was here in Boston that Booth met sixteen-year-old Isabel Sumner, and a clandestine love affair developed between the two. Although she lived just a few blocks from the Tremont Hotel where he stayed, did Isabel meet him at the stage door, as many have theorized, or at the home of Massachusetts Senator Charles Sumner, her father's cousin?

There is no evidence showing that there was a connection between

Isabel and the Senator; however, later generations of the family recall the relationship.[68] If so, is this where the assassination plot materialized? Senator Sumner, if you'll recall, was the Radical Republican with everything to gain from Lincoln's death.

Over the course of the affair, Booth presented Isabel with lavish gifts of a pearl ring with the inscription "J. W. B. to I. S." and a copy of his portrait bearing his autograph, "Yours With Affection, John Wilkes Booth." In addition, a receipt has been found dated May 31, 1864, stating: "This is to certify that the undersigned has purchased the dressing gown from Mrs. Wilson for seventy-five dollars and which is paid this date. 31 May 1864, J. Wilkes Booth."[69] Isabel was born on May 31 or June 1, 1847. Did this receipt represent a birthday gift from her lover?

Six letters have been recovered from Booth to Isabel, but none from her to Booth. In these letters, he expresses his love for her but earnestly requests that she not show them to anybody—ever. Why? Because she just turned seventeen? In the mid-1800s, many seventeen-year-old teenagers already had a brood running around their house. True, Booth was also secretly dating Radical Republican John Hale's daughter Lucy, to whom he would eventually become engaged, but was another reason for secrecy to keep all suspicions away from the Sumners and Hales? Many historians believe that Booth met with the Confederate Secret Service at the Parker House in Boston in July. On July 24, Booth wrote to Isabel, "Remember, dear friend, not to let anyone see my letters. I will come at once to Boston."[70] Was his Parker House "meeting" two days later simply a tryst with Isabel Sumner and a business/conspiracy meeting with Charles Sumner?

John Wilkes Booth was without a doubt a southern sympathizer,

Charles Sumner. Mathew Brady, between 1855 and 1865.

who passionately hated blacks and abolitionists and actively aided the Confederate cause. But connecting the dots shows inexplicably that he was simply a pawn used in a much larger conspiracy to change the face of the United States government for profiteering purposes:

- There is almost no doubt that Lafayette Baker and Secretary of War Stanton knew of the impending assassination.
- Senator John Hale, Booth's fiancée's father, visited President Lincoln at the White House on the morning of the assassination. Later that morning, Booth was seen talking with Lucy in the lobby of the National Hotel. Was this when Booth learned that Lincoln would be attending the performance at Ford's Theatre that night?
- John F. Parker was one of four Washington police officers hired to protect the president by Lafayette Baker. His job history included a charge of conduct unbecoming an officer and drunkenness while on duty. Not surprisingly, Parker was assigned to guard the president the night of April 14. After President Lincoln and Mrs. Lincoln were seated, Parker assumed his position just outside the state box. Soon after the play *Our American Cousin* began, Parker left his station for a seat in the theater where he could both see and hear the play. At intermission, he and two others left the theater for the saloon next door and were not seen again until the next morning. On May 1, Parker was charged with dereliction of duty. He was tried on May 3, and the complaint was dismissed. No transcripts or newspaper articles exist, and Parker remained on the police force for another three years.
- Boston Corbett, John Wilkes Booth's murderer, was not your typical US cavalryman. A highly religious man who was tempted too often by prostitutes, Corbett castrated himself with a pair of scissors, then went to a prayer meeting, ate a full meal, and took a walk. But he did eventually wind up in Massachusetts General Hospital.[71] As we've seen, following the shooting of Booth, Corbett was charged, placed under technical arrest, and released by Secretary of War Edwin Stanton.

Although no concrete proof exists, there's very little doubt that Corbett was Stanton's Jack Ruby, ordered to kill Booth if he were taken alive. If a suffocating Booth had run from the burning barn, there certainly was the chance he would have been taken into custody and returned to Washington, where (like Lee Harvey Oswald) he would have had the opportunity to implicate political and financial conspirators.

- Senator John Hale (whose request to be ambassador to Spain had been approved by President Lincoln) and his daughter Lucy were preparing for their departure. Co-conspirator David Herold also planned to be in Spain. Is there any doubt where Booth expected to be? Both he and Herold were probably headed for a southern port to board a blockade runner for England to collect their payoff, and from there proceed to Spain.

- An intense investigation followed the assassination, with eighteen hundred people interviewed. But the one person who knew John Wilkes Booth probably more intimately than anyone else in his adult years, who spent a portion of the morning of the assassination with him in full view of dozens of people in the National Hotel lobby, and who could probably have shed some additional light into his motives and actions, was never questioned—Lucy Hale.

- Lincoln assassination experts James O. Hall and Michael Maione document very interesting facts regarding the money trail of the co-conspirators:
  1. Atzerodt reportedly bragged that he and others were about to commit something that would either get them hanged on the spot or make them very rich.
  2. David Herold bragged to friends that soon he would be in Spain, and that if he ever came back, he would be rich enough to buy the whole town.[72]

- Booth earned a lot as an actor, reportedly between $300 and $900 per week, quite a sum for anyone in the mid-nineteenth century. But he also lost a lot of money in investments. Joseph H. Simonds, Booth's business agent, testified at the trial of the conspirators that Booth took a $6,000 loss in his Pennsylvania oil business.[73] He would not have had the fortune required to pay the conspirators their fee, and as we've already seen, the Confederacy was in debt up to its ears. The only probable and reasonable source of guaranteed payment for the assassins was from the British and/or the money interests of the North, possibly funneled through Stanton and Wilson.

Possibly the most astonishing discovery pertaining to the Lincoln assassination was made by Indiana State University Professor Ray A. Neff in April 1957 at Leary's Book Store in Philadelphia. Searching for anything interesting on the Civil War, he purchased the May through August 1864 issues of *Colburn's United Service Magazine and Military Journal*. Noticing that some of the pages contained penciled-in figures and letters along the margins that appeared to be a cipher, Neff showed them to a cryptography expert, who confirmed his suspicions and offered deciphering instructions. The startling details are included in Neff and Leonard F. Guttridge's 2003 *Dark Union: The Secret Web of Profiteers, Politicians, and Booth Conspirators That Led to Lincoln's Death*:

> "It was on the tenth of April sixty-five when I first knew that the plan was in action." What followed was a detailed charge that Abraham Lincoln's Secretary of War had fostered a plot hatched among influential persons in the North to have the president kidnapped and, if necessary, killed . . . "I know the truth and it frightens me. I fear that somehow I may become the sacrificial goat. There were at least eleven members of Congress involved in the plot, no less than twelve army officers, three naval officers and at least 24 civilians, of which one was a governor of a loyal state. Five were bankers of great repute, three were nationally known newspapermen and eleven were industrialists of great wealth . . . Eighty-five thousand dollars [S. H. Note: approximately $1.1 million in today's currency] was contributed by the named persons to pay for the deed. Only eight persons knew the details of the plot and the identity of the others . . . I fear for my

life, LCB." Further expert testing verified that the signature and writing was that of Lafayette Charles Baker.[74]

Baker apparently died from meningitis in 1868, just eighteen months after his allegations, leading to the suggestion that he was permanently silenced. Utilizing modern technology, Neff analyzed several strands of Baker's hair, determining that he died from arsenic poisoning. Baker's wife kept a diary, which states that her brother Wally Pollack, *a War Department employee*, brought Baker beer on several occasions. Could the beer have been laced with arsenic?[75]

Congressmen, bankers, industrialists of great wealth, and a governor apparently hired John Wilkes Booth to kill the president of the United States, his vice president, and his Secretary of State on April 14, 1865. One day later, Senate President Pro Tempore Lafayette S. Foster would have been sworn into office as the temporary POTUS, awaiting the election of a new administration—most likely Ulysses S. Grant and Edwin Stanton. Atzerodt and Herold most likely would have pocketed around $40,000 combined if they had survived, with Booth keeping most of everything remaining.

As for Southern Reconstruction, President Andrew Johnson rejected the Radicals, calling for amnesty of the former Confederate slave owners and military. The Radicals, though, were able to muster up a majority in the 1866 congressional races and pushed through much of the needed legislation they required.

It was the prevention of the potential of Lincoln's monetary policy that was the big winner for the bankers and the wealthy industrialists. If Lincoln had continued his greenback policy in establishing a debt-free currency, these bankers would not have been able to establish the Federal Reserve System, and the industrialists most likely would not have been able to build their fortunes to such staggering degrees.

Even if Booth had failed, Abraham Lincoln's life would most likely have come to an end. There was very little possibility that the Northern and British bankers, and the Radical Republicans, were going to allow his expected monetary and southern economic reconstruction policies to exist. One of our great presidents, who though sometimes unconstitutionally ran the country in what he considered its best interests during wartime, had no chance of making that same Constitution stand for what the founders meant it to be.

Lincoln fought the Civil War to preserve the Union. That task now behind him, his desire was to mend the rift with a reconstruction that benefited all. But those same forces in the North that caused the War Between the States, burned even brighter before the last shot was fired. In the actual reconstruction following the assassination, profits by the entrepreneurs from our resources soared, investors and creditors revamped our banking and monetary system to suit their own ends, cheap immigrant labor manned the factories, the military was used to put down labor strikes, and the budding railroads were given a hundred million acres for free.

Reconstruction by the post–Lincoln politicians and financial sector reduced the South to subservience to the North. The country's economic structure was designed to serve the northern industrialists and financial centers. State legislatures that tried to protect their people from predatory capitalists were thwarted by the Supreme Court, which decided that corporations were persons protected by the due process clause of the Fourteenth Amendment. Besides the obvious political payback for his presidency, it is easy to see why Ulysses S. Grant placed Edwin Stanton on the Supreme Court in 1868.

Before the Civil War, a fortune was a few hundred thousand dollars; after the Reconstruction period, the so-called robber barons amassed millions. Henry Wilson, the pro-British, consummate Radical Republican, and vice president under Grant, once said that the Republican Party was "created by no man or set of men but brought into being by almighty God himself . . . and endowed by the creator with all political power and every office under Heaven."[76]

1881: The Assassination of President James Garfield—The First Successful Coup d'état in American History

President James A. Garfield's assassination, published in 1881 in *Frank Leslie's Illustrated Newspaper*. Garfield is supported by Secretary of State James G. Blaine. At left, assassin Charles Guiteau is restrained by members of the crowd. A. Berghaus and C. Upham, published in *Frank Leslie's Illustrated Newspaper*, 1881.

Everyone was taken completely by surprise when James Garfield won the Republican Party nomination for twentieth president of the United States. The nomination was supposed to go to former president Ulysses S. Grant, but the first thirty-five ballots were deadlocked. On the thirty-sixth ballot, Garfield—who had received just one or two courtesy votes on each roll call—unexpectedly received the support of the remaining candidates.

Then Garfield was elected president, squeaking by to win the popular vote by almost ten thousand votes, much to the chagrin of the industrialists and money powers. They were now faced with a president who believed in hard money (currency backed by gold so it retains its value), and who had unpardonably appointed Minnesota's William Windom as his treasury secretary, insisting that he wanted someone free from the influence of the Eastern bankers. Furthermore, Garfield immediately established himself as the undisputed party leader, ignoring senatorial courtesy as a way of appointing individuals to key positions, one of the methods used by lobbyists to gain influence in key areas of the nation's government during each presidency. For potentially the next eight years, they would have to do without that important luxury.

So just a mere hundred days after taking office, President James Garfield was shot in the back at a train station, one more independent president who could not be controlled.

1898: The Spanish-American War—Manifest Destiny Leaves the Continental US for the First Time

B y the late 1800s, national territorial expansion was over. The railroads were built, and the supply chains were completed. Business was good, profits were there, but real corporate growth was no longer a reality. Other markets were needed for the country's wealth and power to reach new heights. Lo and behold, the Cuban situation would be the road toward the emerging markets of Asia and Central America.

Born in 1863, William Randolph Hearst was the son of George Hearst, one of the richest men in America when the Civil War began. In 1887, George accepted the *San Francisco Examiner* as payment for a gambling debt, and his son became the proprietor. Through the years, the young Hearst became a newspaper and magazine magnate, acquiring the likes of the *Chicago Examiner*, *Cosmopolitan*, and *Harper's Bazaar*. Besides building a castle in San Simeon, California, on a quarter million-acre ranch, William Randolph Hearst is probably best remembered for helping to inspire and ignite the Spanish-American War.

Newspaper columnist Ernest L. Meyer wrote, "Mr. Hearst in his long and not laudable career has inflamed Americans against Spaniards, Americans against Japanese, Americans against Filipinos, Americans against Russians, and in the pursuit of his incendiary campaign he has printed downright lies, forged documents, faked atrocity stories, inflammatory editorials, sensational cartoons and photographs and other devices by which he abetted his jingoistic ends."[77]

Hearst purchased the *New York Journal* in 1895 and promptly came into stiff competition with Joseph Pulitzer's *New York World*. This rivalry had an enormous impact on the beginning of the Spanish-American War, which for all intents and purposes permanently dissolved the Spanish Empire, and gave Cuba, Hawaii, the Philippines, Guam, and Puerto Rico to the United States. America emerged as an international player, now with a foothold in Latin America and East Asia. And although the explosion and subsequent sinking of the USS *Maine* in Cuba's harbor was the final straw, Hearst and Pulitzer's yellow journalism paved the way.

Named after *The Yellow Kid* comic strip featured in both newspapers, Hearst and Pulitzer were staunch rivals, each one trying to outdo the other with sensational stories to draw circulation. At one point, Hearst reduced the cost of the paper to a penny, with Pulitzer immediately following suit. As sales increased, so did the public's appetite for

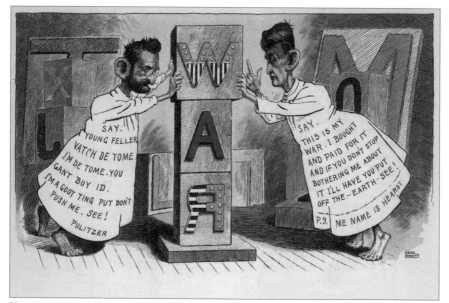

Newspaper publishers Joseph Pulitzer and William Randolph Hearst, full-length, dressed as the Yellow Kid (a popular cartoon character of the day), each pushing against opposite sides of a pillar of wooden blocks that spells WAR. This is a satire of the Pulitzer and Hearst newspapers' role in drumming up USA public opinion to go to war with Spain. Leon Barritt, 1898.

the sensational. Readers almost seemed to beg for new scandals, and the publishers accommodated.

The Cuban insurrection was the event that brought yellow journalism to a fever pitch. The rebels had fought bitterly for years against their Spanish rulers, and the *Journal* fervently declared its support. Hearst even refused to carry any news from the Spanish side, saying that only the revolutionaries could be trusted, turning the conflict into the Spanish villains versus the Cuban rebel heroes— probably the first example of good versus evil to inspire Americans for war.

There was no doubt Spain was oppressing Cuba with harsh rule, even placing many in concentration camps. But the two newspapers took advantage of it, with headlines plastered across newsstands such as "SPANISH CANNIBALISM" and "INHUMAN TORTURE." In his memoir, James Creelman, a fan of Hearst, states that after *Journal* correspondent Frederick Remington arrived in Cuba to report on the conflict, he wrote back asking to return home since there were no signs of war. Creelman claims that Hearst replied, "Please remain. You furnish the pictures, I'll furnish the war." Presumably intended to compliment Hearst by showing the verve of yellow journalism, it most likely was a fabricated account since no source has ever been shown.[78] It certainly illustrates how Hearst helped to precipitate a war.

Then, on February 15, 1898, three weeks after she arrived on a friendly visit, 260 US sailors were killed when an explosion rocked the USS *Maine* docked in Havana Harbor. Most newspapers called for patience and vigilance toward any US response, but the *World* and *Journal* published inflammatory rhetoric. Two days later, the *Journal's* front page featured headlines offering a "$50,000 reward for the conviction of the criminals . . . Naval officers think the Maine was destroyed by a Spanish mine. . . ."[79] The *World* claimed to have sold five million newspapers that week, and the public clamored for President McKinley to declare war. Editorials demanded that the United States act accordingly to avenge the deaths. The slogan "Remember the *Maine*! To hell with Spain!" echoed at the dinner table and in the Capitol and White House.

An inquiry immediately following the sinking concluded that the *Maine* was destroyed by an external explosion that triggered a subsequent magazine explosion. The official story of an external explosion eliminated the possibility that it was caused by an internal accident or sabotage from within. So, who blew it up? The Spanish government? Cuban rebels? Accidentally, by an old Spanish mine that somehow drifted into the harbor? The Weylerites, Spanish right-wing radicals who committed atrocities against the Cubans and were subsequently replaced by the government?

There was no geyser-like spout immediately following the explosion, and there were no dead fish floating around the ship. Both of those events almost certainly would have been likely signs of an external explosion. The AP, via the *Humboldt Times* on February 17, 1898, reported that "Most of the naval officers believe the explosion resulted from a spontaneous explosion in the coal bunkers. . . . Also listed as possible causes were a boiler explosion or overheating of an iron partition between the boilers and the ship's ammunition magazine."[80]

We'll probably never know with any certainty how those 260 American sailors perished. But we do know that due to the sinking of the USS *Maine* and the subsequent three-month war, the United States became a world power, with a gateway to South and Central America via the Caribbean islands, and in the Pacific Ocean, oh so close to the Asian continent.

In April 1898, The United States Senate passed the Teller Amendment as an addition to the resolution of war which disclaimed any intention of the United States to exercise any jurisdiction over Cuba and asserted America's determination to leave the government and control of the country to the Cuban people. In 1902, the Senate passed the Platt Amendment, which stated that US consent must be given for all Cuban treaties and trade agreements, and the United States was given "the right to intervene for the preservation of Cuban independence, the maintenance of a government adequate for the protection of life, property. . . ."[81] It took America less than four years to reverse itself.

In 1890, United States investments in Cuba totaled $50 million, roughly 7 percent of all US foreign trade. Already by the 1880s, American capital was heavily invested in the Cuban economy and all the islands in the Caribbean, especially the sugar industry. The United States even offered Spain $100 million ($2.5 billion in today's currency) to buy Cuba, a mere pittance compared to its actual worth. The Spaniards said no.

Cuban rebels were doing exactly what the Viet Cong accomplished more than a half century later. They were beating a highly experienced and well-equipped army, and in 1898, victory was near. America not only couldn't, they wouldn't allow the Cuban rebels to win and seize control of their country. It was in the best economic interests of America not to have a sovereign Cuba. The United States government never recognized Cuba's fight or its right to independence. It never recognized the Cuban people's struggle as a legitimate force. In his message to Congress on April 11, 1898, asking for war with Spain, President McKinley stated, "Nor from the standpoint of expediency do I think it would be wise or prudent for this Government to recognize at the present time the independence of the so-called Cuban Republic."[82]

The leaders of the Cuban revolution met on November 10, 1898, in order to establish a new government. The United States recognized neither the commission nor the government, stating that the war with Spain was a result of the sinking of the USS *Maine*, not to liberate Cuba.[83]

- The Cubans were excluded from peace talks with Spain.
- The United States simply became the new ruler and colonizer, as the Platt Amendment confirmed four years later.
- When the last Spanish troops departed Cuba, it was the American flag that was hanging in Havana.[84]

Within six hours, Commodore George Dewey's squadron sunk the entire Spanish fleet in Manila Bay, the Philippines.

Unlike the Cubans, the Filipinos did not accept American occupation, fighting a bloody revolutionary war until July of 1902. United States interests were obvious. In addition to being a new market for American goods and investment dollars, the Philippines happens to be just seven hundred miles from China. Besides financial gain, the Philippines would provide the use of military bases in the Pacific, within easy range of the Asian mainland. This would be the initial wedge into Asia, for the expansion of American businesses and banks. In late 1902, just after the fall of the Filipino revolutionaries, the

Filipino casualties on the first day of Philippine-American War. Original caption is "Insurgent dead just as they fell in the trench near Santa Ana, February 5th. The trench was circular, and the picture shows but a small portion." Unknown US Army soldier or employee, 1899.

National City Bank opened its first branch in Manila. Possession of the Philippines by the United States changed the entire power base in the Far East.

United States Assistant Secretary of the Treasury Frank A. Vanderlip—soon-to-be president of the National City Bank and one of the architects of the Federal Reserve—said:

> It is as a base for commercial operations that the islands seem to possess the greatest importance. They occupy a favored location not with reference to one part of any particular country of the Orient, but to all parts. Together with the islands of the Japanese Empire, since the acquirement of Formosa, the Philippines are the pickets of the Pacific, standing guard at the entrances to trade with the millions of China and Korea, French Indo-China, the Malay Peninsula and the Islands of Indonesia to the south.[85]

Captain Alfred T. Mahan, head of the Naval War College and a leading expansionist, reasoned that America's survival depended upon a strong navy and the acquisition of island possessions to be used as naval bases in the Pacific. The time was ripe, Mahan preached, for Americans to turn their "eyes outward, instead of inward only, to seek the welfare of the country."[86] Out of Mahan's lectures grew two major works on the historical significance of sea power. In these volumes he argues that naval power was the key to success in international politics. The country that controlled the seas would control modern warfare. Theodore Roosevelt and others who believed that a big navy and overseas expansion were vital to the nation's welfare were greatly influenced by his writings. Controlling the Pacific would necessitate the need for the creation of a true two-ocean navy, which would also necessitate the development of a canal across Central America.

This was a well-oiled machinery from top to bottom, taking America into a position of world dominance, especially with regard to Latin America and Asia. For several years, Pulitzer and Hearst bandied back and forth, exciting the citizenry into a crazed frenzy against the imagined Spanish tyrants. Then, right before the Cubans were about to claim victory and independence from foreign control (as Fidel Castro succeeded in doing a half century later), 260 sailors most likely became casualties of war so that the legislators and the president could begin the assimilation of sovereign territories, with the military pulling off an invasion on two fronts with a precision that was most likely the envy of every other navy in the world. If the USS *Maine* had not exploded, the wealth and power of the United States would not have increased exponentially throughout Asia and Central and South America in the years prior to World War I.

A late twentieth-century investigation concluded that the probable cause of the loss of the *Maine* was a boiler problem. Whether or not that "problem" was sabotage will almost certainly never be known. What we do know, however, is that "Remember the *Maine*!" was the American slogan used for the acquisition of Guam, Hawaii, the Philippines, Puerto Rico, the control over the Cuban people and economy for a half century, and the permanent occupation of Guantanamo Bay for military purposes, all in the name of freeing

OUTLINE MAP SHOWING THE TERRITORY OF GREATER AMERICA.

Shows territories and possessions of the United States after the Spanish American War, including Alaska, Cuba, Hawaii, Marianas, Philippines, Puerto Rico, and Samoa in addition to the continental United States. Printed in the book *War in the Philippines* by Marshall Everet, 1899.

the Cuban citizenry from the Spanish monsters. And in the process, almost three hundred thousand died, including over two hundred thousand Filipino citizens. The Spanish-American War and its aftermath planted the seed for the ravages of the next century.

Political satire showing Manifest Destiny bringing the children of Uncle Sam's new American states and country acquisitions into America's fold, assimilating their population. Keppler, Udo J., 1898.

December 23, 1913: The Federal Reserve Act

Is Signed into Law

"Whoever controls the volume of money in any country is absolute master of all industry and commerce."—US President James A. Garfield, assassinated just 100 days into his presidency

"The [Federal Reserve] Banks are listed neither as 'wholly owned' government corporations . . . nor as 'mixed ownership' corporations. . . . Additionally, Reserve Banks, as privately-owned entities, receive no appropriated funds from Congress. . . . Finally, the Banks are empowered to sue and be sued in their own name. . . . They carry their own liability insurance and typically process and handle their own claims. In the past, the Banks have defended against tort claims directly, through private counsel, not government attorneys. . . . For these reasons we hold that the Reserve Banks are not federal agencies. . . ."
—Lewis vs. United States, 680 F. 2d 1239 9th Circuit 1982

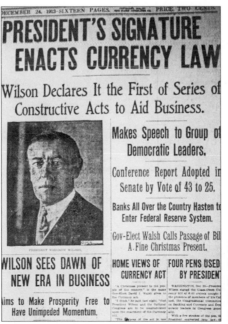

Newspaper clipping
USA, Woodrow Wilson
signs creation of the
Federal Reserve,
December 24, 1913.

It took more than a century, but at 6 p.m. on December 23, 1913, America's central banking system, The Federal Reserve Act, was signed into law by President Woodrow Wilson. The American economy and its currency were now totally controlled by "the Fed," which had the means to fluctuate inflationary or deflationary conditions at their whim via interest rates, by placing money into circulation by selling interest-bearing notes (known recently as "quantitative easing"), and introducing the American banking system to fractional reserve banking which artificially increases the money supply.

Though there were a few periods of federal taxation prior to the Federal Reserve System, American citizens generally paid zero taxes. Federal and state expenses were paid for primarily through tariffs. But the US government would need income to pay the interest owed to pay its creditors, thanks to the huge national debt soon to be incurred due to Federal Reserve monetary policies. In addition, social services such as welfare, unemployment, and food stamps—primarily caused by the economic conditions precipitated by the Federal Reserve inflationary and deflationary tactics—had to be paid for as well. So, just a few months prior to the passing of the Federal Reserve Act, Congress passed the Sixteenth Amendment to the US Constitution, now making it legal to collect federal income tax from American citizens.

The Fed runs America's economy and currency—simple as that. Economic growth and stock market decreases generally occur when the Fed increases interest rates. When they deflate money and credit, the economy retracts and slows, and stock market "corrections" occur. American jobs, a family's spending ability, and retirement savings are all totally controlled by a private corporation having absolutely no allegiance to the country, with not one sitting president or member of Congress ever witnessing a Federal Reserve meeting to hear how the country's economic policy is being decided, or to lend its input as the people's representatives.

Every American taxpayer, including their president and congressmen, should ask why the Federal Reserve was not constructed as a government agency and manned by government employees, who could be held accountable to our legislators and president. This is tantamount to having Air Force One owned and operated by an airplane manufacturer such as Boeing instead of the United States Air Force. If the Fed was in fact established, as was claimed, to prevent another bank panic like the one in 1907, how did the stock market crash and eventual Great Depression occur less than two decades later, with presumably the greatest financial minds in charge of America's economy and currency?

The official story is that the Federal Reserve was mandated by Congress to "provide for the establishment of Federal reserve banks, to furnish an elastic currency, to afford means of rediscounting commercial paper, to establish a more effective supervision of banking in the United States, and for other purposes. *This will ensure that the American economy remains stable and healthy.*" [Italics inserted by S. H. to add emphasis.] But that's the furthest thing from the truth. The common nickname for the Federal Reserve Bank may be "the Fed" but it should be "the Priv." Although the chairman of the Federal Reserve is appointed to a four-year term by the president with the support and guidance of the Senate, and the chairman reports on the state of the economy to Congress once a year, the Federal Reserve is a totally private banking system making its own monetary decisions and *is not accountable to any branch of the United States government.* The Federal Reserve is a private corporation and, unlike every other government agency, has no subservience to the federal government. The word "federal" was simply placed in its name to give it the appearance of a federal agency. This private corporation is not publicly traded, so no statistics or details of employee ownership are made public.

- Property owned by the Federal Reserve is subject to local property taxes. Government buildings are not taxed.
- The Federal Reserve's salaried employees are not government civil service employees, and they have their own retirement plan.
- All meetings of the Federal Reserve are held in complete secrecy.
- There have never been any minutes reported to Congress or the public, only a summary of the proceedings, usually issued a few weeks following the meeting.

The United States Constitution clearly states that only Congress can coin money, but even though an amendment is the only legal way to alter the Constitution, the Federal Reserve Act took that power away from Congress. Or, rather, Congress illegally relinquished the power to another entity. In his March 4, 1837, farewell address, President Andrew Jackson emphasized what he felt was the potential evil inherent in the paper money system of the Central Bank:

> The immense capital and peculiar privileges bestowed upon it enabled it to exercise despotic sway over the other banks in every part of the country. From its superior strength . . . it openly claimed for itself the power of regulating the currency throughout the United States. In other words, it asserted (and it undoubtedly possessed) the power to make money plenty or scarce, at its pleasure, at any time, and in any quarter of the Union, by controlling the issues of other banks and permitting an expansion or compelling a general contraction of the circulating medium according to its own will . . . *and this organized* money power, *from its secret conclave, would have directed the choice of your highest officers and compelled you to make peace or war as best suited their own wishes. The forms of your government might, for a time, have remained; but its living spirit would have departed from it. . . .*[87] [Italics inserted by S. H. to add emphasis.]

With the national debt projected to be $23 trillion in 2020,[88] Americans have paid almost $11 trillion in interest since 1988.[89] How do the money interests make billions from America's money through the Federal Reserve System, at the full expense of each American, while keeping the country in perpetual debt?

- Article 1, Section 8, Clause 5 of the United States Constitution states that only Congress can coin money and regulate the value of that money, yet the Fed creates it out of thin air. In reality, the United States Congress illegally passed an act of Congress, and it has never been challenged in the Supreme Court.

- If the Fed wishes to increase the money supply, it simply buys securities from security dealers, paying those dealers electronically, with no actual money changing hands. *The Fed electronically creates US currency.* The money is deposited in the banks of the dealers, increasing the money supply, exactly what the Fed did immediately after the 2008 financial crisis with their quantitative easing method. In QE4 (the fourth phase) for instance, every month the bank purchased $85 billion worth of Treasury bonds from their member banks, in effect, coining $85 billion into circulation. Again, constitutionally, only Congress has that power.

- When the Fed wants to fund the government, it takes money out of circulation by selling Treasury bonds to dealers who auction them off.
- All of these transactions increase or decrease a bank's reserves, and when a bank increases its reserves, it can loan more money due to fractional reserve banking.
- The Federal Reserve, at its whim, creates and destroys America's currency.

FRACTIONAL RESERVE BANKING

In the United States, due to the Federal Reserve, only a fraction of a bank's assets are backed by cash deposits. Whatever the Fed determines to be the reserve, usually around 10 percent, is the amount of money that the bank must keep in reserve. If a bank customer deposits $1,000 in their account, the bank keeps $100 "in reserve" and $900 becomes available for the bank to loan to other people. And so on . . . and on—thousands of dollars are created from one $1,000 deposit. Therefore, member banks of the Federal Reserve also create money, again in direct violation of the United States Constitution.

And it gets even weirder if one peruses the Federal Reserve Bank of Chicago's 1982 publication *Modern Money Mechanics: A Workbook on Bank Reserves and Deposit Expansion.* If a bank loans $10,000 it deposits that amount in the recipient's account, but the bank is required to retain only $1,000 of that deposit. The remaining $9,000 excess reserve can be loaned or invested. The book states:

Of course, they [banks] do not really pay out loans from the money they receive as deposits. If they did this, no additional money would be created. What they do when they make loans is to accept promissory notes in exchange for credits to the borrowers' transaction accounts. Loans (assets) and deposits (liabilities) both rise by $9,000. Reserves are unchanged by the loan transactions. But the deposit credits constitute new additions to the total deposits of the banking system.[90]

So, when you take out a loan for $20,000, if the reserve percentage is 10 percent, the bank is enabled to loan out $18,000—in cash! The bank created $18,000 in cash, loaned out that money (minus the reserve), and will receive interest on both loans, all as profit; all as worthless money except to the profits of the banking powers.

All money is created out of nothing, yet without money all trade ends, except for bartering. When you remove money or reduce the supply, the results are catastrophic. Witness the despair of the Great Depression. The exact same infrastructure that existed during the prosperous 1920s was in existence in the 1930s. The same workforce was available, our fertile farmland, our highly efficient transportation system, and a massive communications network were all there. Americans lacked only one item after the Crash of 1929—an adequate supply of money. And because of this, banks refused to make personal and commercial loans, but conversely, all existing debts from pre-Depression loans were due to the banks. People and companies did not have the money to pay those debts, and the banks repossessed homes and businesses, which the banks now owned. Since Congress gave away its power to create currency to the bankers in the Federal Reserve Act, the banks were America's only source of money and credit.

This was America's depression, all caused by a shortage of money, and it could have been cured immediately by the creation of money—the same money being thrown out by the Federal Reserve after the 2008 fiscal crisis (around $85 billion each month, over a trillion each year, in quantitative easing). Instead, the Federal Reserve "foreclosed" on the middle and lower classes after the stock market crash of 1929!

Post–World War II prosperity only came about because there was now an adequate supply of money. A lack of money created the

Depression; an abundant supply ended it. This is how bankers use the Federal Reserve System; this is what they had been fighting for all through the 1800s and finally won in 1913; this is almost assuredly why there was an attempt on President Jackson's life, and this is one of the reasons both Presidents Lincoln and Garfield were assassinated.

During the 1920s and 2000s, thirteen of the world's greatest economic and monetary minds—the Fed chairman and his twelve board members—secretly met eight times a year. How did these brilliant monetary strategists not anticipate the Crash of 1929 and the 2008 fiscal crisis? How did these monetary geniuses who control the financial infrastructure of the country, who control the nation's inflationary and recessionary trends and the ups and downs of the stock market (virtually by their own policies) not see a collapse coming?

Imagine you are Eugene Meyer, chairman of the 1930 Federal Reserve. You see your country devastated by the Great Depression. Corporations fail. One out of every four able-bodied workers is unemployed, unable to feed and clothe their families, and some become homeless. There are starving people on soup lines and great food shortages. Misery is everywhere. As your duty calls, would you not report to the president and Congress that a war must be declared—not one against Germany, or Korea, or Vietnam—but a war against the Great Depression? You would tell them that since a shortage of money started this horror, let's now make it abundant. All that Presidents Hoover and Roosevelt and Eugene Meyer had to do was instruct the Federal Reserve to begin a quantitative easing of buying Treasuries, to institute social programs and construction projects to build up the urban infrastructure and add farming incentives and corporate tax incentives for renewed production and hiring, among other options. True, issuance of Treasuries didn't begin until 1929, so there may not have been enough in circulation to accomplish all financial goals. They found a way, though, to finance World War I, so those great financial minds in the Federal Reserve could have found a way to finance the war against the Great Depression.

As you probably already know, when the average American family takes out a thirty-year mortgage on a $250,000 home, they will pay back roughly $1million dollars (about three-quarters of a million in interest plus the principal.) But if they sell, which many do, whether two or ten years later, they will have paid mostly interest, with very little principal. They then usually purchase a more expensive home, and the cycle begins again. American homeowners pay interest on their mortgage loans based on a thirty-year loan, yet many have that loan for only a relatively brief period. Why don't they receive interest rebates when they sell their home after five years based on a five-year loan?

What's even worse is that the Federal Reserve controls the housing market. When they decrease interest rates, it's a boon; and at their whim, they increase the rates high enough to cause the market to drop. And since homes are the backbone of the average American family, just a handful of people control the lives of the average American.

History tells us of debt-free and interest-free money issued by governments. The American colonies did it in the 1700s, and their wealth soon rivaled England's and brought restrictions from Parliament, which led to the Revolutionary War. Abraham Lincoln did it in 1863 to help finance the Civil War and was later assassinated. Germany issued debt-free and interest-free money from 1935, helping to account for its startling rise from the depression to a world power so quickly:

> Hitler and the National Socialists, who came to power in 1933, thwarted the international banking cartel by issuing their own money. In this they took their cue from Abraham Lincoln, who funded the American Civil War with government-issued paper money called Greenbacks. . . .
>
> Within two years, the unemployment problem had been solved and the country was back on its feet. It had a solid, stable currency, no debt, and no inflation, at a time when millions of people in the United States and other Western countries were still out of work and living on welfare.[91]

1900–1917: The Military Goes to Work
Protecting America's Sphere of Influence

Brigadier General Smedley Butler, Official USMC photograph, 1927.

The first known American war hero to recognize America's war machine was Major General Smedley Darlington Butler, United States Marine Corp. Butler was awarded two Congressional Medals of Honor for the capture of Vera Cruz, Mexico, in 1914, and for the capture of Ft. Riviere, Haiti, in 1917. Presented with the Distinguished Service Medal in 1919, he was the most decorated Marine in American history at the time of his death in 1940.

War heroes Audie Murphy and Alvin York appear in American history books and movies, but not Major General Butler, unsurprisingly. You see, following his retirement, Smedley openly expressed his views opposing the American war system, almost assuredly prompting his omission from textbooks and the movie theaters. In his book *War is a Racket*, he exposes the relationship between the money powers and the United States government.

> I spent 33 years and four months in active military service and during that period I spent most of my time as a high-class muscle man for Big Business, for Wall Street and the bankers. In short, I was a racketeer, a gangster for capitalism. I helped make Mexico and especially Tampico safe for American oil interests in 1914. I helped make Haiti and Cuba a decent place for the National City Bank boys to collect revenues in. I helped in the raping of half a dozen Central American republics for the benefit of Wall Street. I helped purify Nicaragua for the International Banking House of Brown Brothers in 1902–1912. I brought light to the Dominican Republic for the American sugar interests in 1916. I helped make Honduras right for the American fruit companies in 1903. In China in 1927, I helped see to it that Standard Oil went on its way unmolested. Looking back on it, I might have given Al Capone a few hints. The best he could do was to operate his racket in three districts. I operated on three continents. . . .[92]

Rather than establishing colonies or protectorates in the Caribbean and Pacific immediately following the Spanish-American War, America indirectly declared to the world that these lands were off-limits to any other country. Cuba, the Philippines, and many Latin American countries became a part of America's "sphere of influence."

Avoiding the pitfalls and complications of declaring a conquered nation a colony with democratic rights, and the expenses incurred administering a colony, economic and political control was still held by United States corporations, banks, and the government. US battleships and Marines stood ready to protect the dollars. As a matter of fact, in 1921, the Marine Corps brass issued a manual entitled *The Strategy and Tactics of Small Wars*, for the purpose of indoctrinating Marines in how to fight and react properly in future small wars, as they did in Mexico, Haiti, etc.

In 1911, the Dominican Republic's US-supported president was assassinated. Following the election of a new provisional president, President Taft sent some commissioners, along with 750 US Marines. The government promptly stepped down, and a new US-backed government was established.[93] In 1912, the Marines were sent into Nicaragua to put down a revolt. The banking concern Brown Brothers imposed a new loan onto the government, which included an agreement that the country's railroads, customs houses, and its central bank would now be controlled by Brown Brothers. Thousands of Marines were stationed in Nicaragua for thirteen years, sending a message to the rest of the world that the financial and military might of the United States cannot be challenged.[94]

Between 1914 and 1915, the United States used domestic disturbances six times to take control of the Haitian customs houses. When Haiti elected a new president, he refused to hand over the railroads and banks. Smedley was one of the Marines who landed in Port au Prince and seized $500,000, which was immediately transported back to New York and deposited into the National City Bank vaults. Six years later, one of the bank executives testified before the Senate that the purpose of this was to force Haiti into accepting the usual custom house arrangement.[95]

These so-called "banana republics" were forced into economic subservience by America's military might for the profit and continued existence of America's banks and corporations. They are just some of the countries around the world that have been placed into America's sphere of influence.

1918: The Treaty of Versailles Ending World War I Was a Plan for a Second World War

German mass protest at the Reichstag against the signing of the Treaty of Versailles (the brutal peace). Bildarchiv Preußischer Kulturbesitz, May 15, 1919.

Worl War I did nothing for the people of the United States. It did not protect their sovereignty and, although the 1920s was a period of prosperity, it did not improve their lot in life. But it produced 21,000 new American millionaires, and the industrialists became even wealthier by supplying the Allies with necessary war goods and loans and, ultimately, the US war machine. Our allies in Europe were so depleted by war's end that their gold reserves and industrial capacity were now largely dependent on the United States, which controlled almost all of it. As always, the war simply fed the nation's wealth and power, while maiming and killing thousands.

Although powers in the government were possibly quite influential in the yellow journalism of Hearst and Pulitzer, World War I was the first time that a government-sponsored effort controlled the mood of the population. On April 13, 1917, President Wilson used the power of propaganda to fuel public fear and hatred of the German people when he assigned yellow journalist George Creel to head up the Committee on Public Information to garner support for World War I. Roughly ten million Americans hailed from the Central Powers

George Creel, Chairman of the Committee on Public Information. US National Archives and Records Administration, 1918.

that the United States would be fighting, and millions more were Irish-Americans who hated the British. Wilson desperately needed a united America and ordered Creel to garner that support.

And he did, by placing pro-war advertisements in magazines, distributing seventy-five million pamphlets defending the war, and launching a massive campaign for war bonds. He had "four-minute men" excite audiences in theaters with war rallies and encouraged film-makers to produce pro-war movies. And once war broke out, attempts at suppressing German culture in US cities began. German newspapers were closed, and the German language was no longer taught in our schools. Lutheran churches stopped presenting their services in German. Musicians ceased playing Beethoven and Bach, sauerkraut was renamed "liberty cabbage," and the German measles became known as "liberty measles." This fear and hatred of the German population spawned vigilante attacks, and the courts frequently found accused defendants of violence not guilty. St. Louis, with a large German-American population, was asked by one of its newspapers "to wipe out everything German in this city."[96]

The most hideous incident resulting from this anti-German propaganda machine was committed against twenty-nine-year-old German-born bakery employee Robert Prager. Accused of making "disloyal utterances," he was arrested, and an angry mob dragged him out of jail and hanged him from a tree. Allowed to write a note just before being lynched, Prager wrote, "Dear Parents: I must on this, the 4th day of April 1918, die. Please pray for me, my dear parents." During the trial of the perpetrators, the defendants wore ribbons of red, white, and blue, and a band in the courtroom played patriotic songs. The jury deliberated only twenty-five minutes before delivering a not-guilty verdict.[97]

The reason given as to why World War II occurred is Hitler's attack on Poland in 1939, and his determination to rule the world. Yet World War II almost certainly would not have occurred if the Allies had granted Germany an honorable peace, exactly as was given to Japan following World War II. Instead, Germany was left disgraced and in economic ruin, ripe for a despot to come along and sweep it away in his arms. Although there were twenty-seven countries represented at Versailles, the United States, England, and France dominated the peace talks. Yet they weren't peace negotiations, since the Germans were refused a delegation in Paris, along with Austria, Bulgaria, Turkey, and Hungary. The Paris peace talks were simply a list of demands drawn up by the Allies that Germany and the other belligerents had to sign or be invaded and torn apart.

Prior to the war, Austria-Hungary attacked Serbia, and the domino effect of defense treaties drew one nation after another into the conflict. Germany was certainly not an innocent bystander, and was the Allies' dominant foe, inflicting millions of casualties both on land and sea, occupying France, and conducting countless bombing raids on the British Isles. Yet if the US, England, and France truly wanted a lasting peace as they did with Japan following World War II, they would not have devastated the German people with the demands the Treaty of Versailles made on its government:

- Under Article 231, Germany accepted sole responsibility for causing the war, even though it was Austria-Hungary that precipitated hostilities.
- Germany had to pay for all civilian damage caused during the war, with the final bill presented by the Allies on May 1, 1921. In the meantime, the German government had to pay $5 billion in today's currency, with the remainder paid over thirty years.
- Germany would have to ship enormous quantities of coal to Belgium, France, and Italy for ten years.
- Germany agreed to bear the cost of the Allied occupation armies.
- Germany had to agree to the sale of German property in Allied countries to help defray their financial commitment.
- The German Army did not have to surrender, which would have signaled defeat, and was left intact. This was a calculated move.[98]

The war reparations plank was written by John Foster Dulles, future secretary of state under President Eisenhower, causing untold harm to the German people in the years following the war:

- In effect, the German middle class was put on the road to destruction.
- The German mark became hyperinflated.
- It eased the way for a maniac to come to power who unfortunately had the know-how to end inflation like Adolf Hitler, whipping the German people into a nationalistic frenzy.

A member of the British delegation, famed British economist John Maynard Keynes stated, "The peace is outrageous and impossible, and can bring nothing but misfortune behind it."[99] That misfortune turned out to be the Holocaust and World War II.

Even General Pershing could not understand why the German army was not forced to admit defeat. What was the ulterior motive of the Allies who conceived this plan? As it turned out, it was easy for Hitler to blame the Jews and Marxists for the war defeat and not the army or the war machine. He called the German politicians who signed the treaty the "November Criminals." The treaty's terms were so harsh they almost guaranteed there would be another war. In President Herbert Hoover's biography of President Wilson, he quotes Ray Stannard Baker who oversaw Wilson's Press Bureau, referring to the Germans signing the Peace Treaty: "If they do," he wrote, "it will be with crossed fingers. I can see no real peace in it. They have tempered justice with no mercy." Hoover further writes, "Even the president said to me, 'If I were a German, I think I should never sign it.'"[100]

The United States Senate never ratified the treaty.

The Great Depression

The aftermath of World War I was no different for the economy than following World War II—economic prosperity. The automobile, radio, and other new innovations spurred the economy to unprecedented heights, with renewed interest in the stock market for the average citizen to make tons of money—something nearly impossible to realize prior to World War I. Interest in the stock market became so intense that brokers sold stocks on margin, with the investor only having to put down 10 or 20 percent. In other words, if an investor wished to buy $1,000 of US Steel stock, they simply had to have $100 or $200. The broker put up the rest! Citizens were actually allowed to enter the market by borrowing 80 or 90 percent of the value of the stock with money that had to be paid back to the broker if the stock fell below a certain price.

This is eerily similar to the millions of sub-prime mortgages sold prior to the 2008 financial collapse to mostly middle-class homeowners who couldn't afford them. Investor money put into the market did exactly what it was supposed to do—create a market bubble by overpricing stocks, exactly what the 401K investment monies did in the 1990s and 2000s which fed into the 2008 fiscal crisis, creating tremendous losses to middle class retirement funds.

The Dow Jones Industrial Average reached a then all-time high of 381 on September 3, 1929, slightly less than two months prior to the

Crash, when the lives of millions of investors were effectively ruined. True, many companies were beginning to report disappointing earnings, and the economy was certainly slowing, but think about this: In just under two months, from September 3 to October 29, the market fell from 381 down to 230, a 151 points loss, gobbling up 40 percent of the wealth in the market, and beginning the domino effect of companies cutting back, unemployment growing, banks closing, and a massive loss of personal savings. The market had been at a record high, indicating a strong economy, and in just roughly sixty days the money supply entered free-fall. Welcome to the stock market casino.

The Day of Infamy—or Was It the Day of Foreknowledge?

Naval photograph documenting the Japanese attack on Pearl Harbor, Hawaii which initiated US participation in World War II. US Navy caption: The battleship USS *Arizona* sinking after being hit by Japanese air attack on December 7, 1941. US National Archives, December 7, 1941.

President Roosevelt's famous "Day of Infamy" speech following the Japanese attack at Pearl Harbor was characteristic of so many before and after—including McKinley's "Remember the Maine!" and Bush's "Axis of Evil" and "War on Terrorism"—all featuring slogans to rally the American people into war. Soon after World War II ended, Congress and the military conducted several investigations into the Pearl Harbor debacle. How could such a tragedy have occurred? Toward that end, the government declassified a good deal of material in order to conduct its investigation. Not unlike the Warren Commission on JFK's assassination, nothing indicating any wrongdoing was reported by the nine individual commissions.

But George Morgenstern, using the same declassified information, revealed in his 1947 book *Pearl Harbor: The Story of the Secret War* that Pearl Harbor not only could have been avoided but that FDR and his administration *caused* it to happen. A graduate of the University of Chicago, a Marine Corps captain during the war, and an editor at the *Chicago Tribune*, Morgenstern claimed that the United States conducted a "secret war" that was waged in the months and even years leading up to Pearl Harbor:[101] "Four years later it would become known that the Jap secret code had been cracked many months before Pearl Harbor, and that the men in Washington who read the code intercepts had almost as good a knowledge of Japanese plans and intentions as if they had been occupying seats in the war councils of Tokyo."[102]

The Roosevelt Administration knew full well that American servicemen at Pearl Harbor were in harm's way; that attack was imminent—yet neither the island nor the base was ever placed on full military alert.

On January 27, 1941 (ten months prior to Pearl Harbor), United States Ambassador to Japan Joseph C. Grew wrote a memo to his superiors: "A member of the embassy was told by my Peruvian colleague that from many quarters, including a Japanese one, he had heard that a surprise mass attack on Pearl Harbor was planned by the Japanese military forces, in case of "trouble" between Japan and the United States; that the attack would involve the use of all the Japanese military forces. My colleague said that he was prompted to pass this on because it had come to him from many sources, although the plan seemed fantastic."[103] Grew was no clerk sitting at a desk in an FBI office. This was the representative selected by President Franklin Delano Roosevelt to represent the United States of America in one of the world's powerhouse nations at that time.

Roosevelt purposely backed Japan into a corner with economic sanctions, whereby they were forced to go to war:

- On October 16, 1940, the US restricted all sales of scrap iron and steel to all countries except Great Britain and countries in the Western Hemisphere, effectively cutting off Japan's supplies of those crucial metals.
- On July 26, 1941 (just a little more than four months prior to the Pearl Harbor attack), in response to the Japanese occupation of French Indo-China, the US froze all Japanese assets in the United States, effectively ending all trade between the two countries.
- Just one week later, the US cut off all oil sales to Japan, and Britain and the Dutch quickly followed suit. Japan now had access to only approximately 10 percent of its oil requirements.

Japan was in an untenable position with only one way to turn—to war, and the murder of over 2,300 US servicemen and women.

According to noted historian Charles Beard in his *President Roosevelt and the Coming of War*, on February 11, 1941 (nine months prior to Pearl Harbor), FDR proposed sacrificing six cruisers and two aircraft carriers in Manila, Philippines, in order to get America into war with Japan.[104] [S. H. Note: This is reminiscent of Operation Northwoods, which will be discussed later.] The commander of the Pearl Harbor destroyers, Admiral Robert Theobald, argues in *The Final Secret of Pearl Harbor* that Roosevelt deliberately withheld information from the commanders at Pearl Harbor, never alerting them to the imminent attack.

The recurrent fact of the true Pearl Harbor story has been the repeated withholding of information from Admiral Kimmel and General Short. If the War and Navy Departments had been free to follow the dictates of the Art of War, the following is the minimum of information and orders those officers would have received:

. . . On November 28, the Chief of Naval Operations should have ordered Admiral Kimmel to recall the Enterprise from the Wake operation, and a few days later should have directed the cancellation of the contemplated sending of the Lexington to Midway.

As has been repeatedly said, not one word of this information and none of the foregoing orders were sent to Hawaii.

Everything that happened in Washington on Saturday and Sunday, December 6 and 7, supports the belief that President Roosevelt had directed that no message be sent to the Hawaiian Commanders before noon on Sunday, Washington time.[105]

Exactly as Lord Curzon had predicted immediately after World War I, the world again went to war. And once again, the American people were almost totally united in their staunch desire to remain neutral. And, again, the United States government made sure that their soldiers would follow the flag into battle with the full support of its populace.

Pearl Harbor became the second time the United States government used mass trauma to incite the public through terror. (The third if you count the sinking of the *Lusitania* in 1915.) It was the only way FDR could renege on his 1940 campaign pledge not to involve Americans in the European war. By December 8, when Roosevelt asked Congress to declare war on Japan, the public's isolationist philosophy had been replaced by fear and hatred of the Japanese. President Roosevelt and the United States government methodically and meticulously prepared the American people for war.

The Communist Threat

A Huey helicopter sprays Agent Orange over Vietnam. Originally from US Army Operations in Vietnam R. W. Trewyn, PhD, Unknown date.

I t must have taken all the self-control that they could muster for Stalin and Khrushchev not to have doubled over laughing as they watched newsreels of American schoolchildren in the 1950s being herded under classroom desks in monthly nuclear bomb attack drills, and homeowners around the country building fallout shelters, while the USSR's nuclear program was in its infancy. Yes, they had conducted hydrogen bomb testing earlier than expected, and they did have delivery systems capable of reaching the United States. But in 1955, the United States had 2,422 nuclear warheads while the Soviet Union had 200.[106] Panic was the furthest thing that should have been instilled in the American mind. Yet the US government sent panicked schoolchildren scurrying under desks and increased defense spending to unprecedented peacetime levels to build more warheads, missiles, et al.

While the government instilled fear against the hated Commies, détente with Russia was closer than ever in the early 1960s, the Cuban Missile Crisis notwithstanding. By placing missiles ninety miles from America's shores, the Russians were simply trying to counter the American airbases in close proximity to their border in Eastern Europe. Few Americans are aware that the Soviet Union and the United States very nearly collaborated on an aggressive action against China in an attempt to prevent the nuclear arms race from spreading. The *Journal of American History* published a 1988 article by Gordon H. Chang of Stanford University, who was a research associate at the university's International Strategic Institute. The article, titled "JFK, China, and the Bomb," states: "As will be shown, the liberal President John F. Kennedy and his closest advisers, in their quest for a nuclear test ban, not only seriously discussed but also actively pursued the possibility of taking military action *with* [author's emphasis] the Soviet Union against China's nuclear installations at least a year and a half earlier." [S. H. Note: approximately the spring of 1962.][107]

Considered by many to be one of our greatest presidents, Ronald Reagan gave a speech to the Veterans of Foreign Wars and stated that the Vietnam War was a noble cause. That noble cause cost the country billions of dollars. All in the name of containing something that would one day self-destruct. Nary, an American citizen, is unaware of the travesty of the Vietnam conflict, although many might not be aware

A US Air Force Boeing B-52D-35-BW Stratofortress (s/n 52-669) dropping bombs over Vietnam. This aircraft was hit by SA-2 surface-to-air missile over North Vietnam during the Linebacker II offensive on December 31, 1972, and crashed in Laos. The crew of six ejected, but only five were rescued. USAF, Circa 1965–1972.

of its extent. Interestingly, the Vietnamese until this day refer to it as the American War, which lasted for roughly eleven years, from 1964 to 1975, even though the conflict itself actually began in 1959. The death toll was staggering, with 1.1 million military personnel dead, including fifty-eight thousand American soldiers (which includes ten thousand non-hostile deaths).[108] There are varying degrees of estimates of civilian casualties, ranging from 400 thousand to 2 million, so it seems fair to suggest that approximately one million civilians died on both sides, including women and children.

Although South Vietnam was an ally of the United States, the South incurred far more firepower from American forces than the North. Many bombs, shells, and land mines unleashed during the war failed to detonate, continuing to decimate the South Vietnamese population after the war. Estimates are that forty-two thousand Vietnamese have died by leftover explosive devices since the war ended in 1975, injuring another sixty-two thousand.[109]

Inhabitants of South Vietnam also suffered from high birth death

Agent Orange Barrels at Johnston Atoll. US Government photograph, circa 1976.

rates, probably due to the extensive use of defoliants such as Agent Orange, and their timber, rice, and fish suffered serious declines. No other country has ever delivered the amount of chemicals in their armaments as the United States did during the Vietnam War in Laos, Cambodia, and Vietnam. In November 1961, President Kennedy authorized the use of chemicals as a limited experimental exercise, only in Operation Ranch Hand, but from 1962 to 1971 approximately 20 percent of South Vietnam was sprayed with eighteen million gallons of chemicals. In addition, with permission from the Laotian government, the US also carried out herbicide spraying in Laos from 1965 to 1969.[110]

According to Red Cross estimates, three million Vietnamese have been affected by dioxin, a contaminant found in the herbicide mixture Agent Orange. At least 150 thousand Vietnamese children have been born with serious birth defects attributed to dioxin, with millions of Americans and Vietnamese still affected in adverse ways. Sprayed up to twenty times the concentration recommended by the manufacturer, millions of acres of farmland and forests were defoliated with Agent Orange, which was finally banned by the United States in 1971.[111]

United States planes dropped 388,000 tons of napalm in the ten-year period from 1963 to 1973. One bomb engulfed 2,500 square

Napalm bombs explode on Viet Cong structures south of Saigon in the Republic of Vietnam. US Air Force, 1965.

yards in flame, and the brutality of it was such that victims' flesh melted from their body. Napalm adheres to the skin, creating a wound so deep that it cannot heal, and when the victim tries to wipe it off, it spreads to other areas of the body.[112] The cost to the American economy for this devastation was $140 billion; closer to a quarter trillion dollars when all non-war related expenses were factored in, such as death benefits.

And yet, believe it or not, it gets even worse. Forgotten by many Americans, the United States expanded this destruction to neighboring Indochinese countries. In 1964, the CIA, in its largest operation ever, began secret bombing missions in Laos. Over the next nine years, approximately two million tons of bombs were dropped in Northern

Laos on the Plain of Jars, killing fifty thousand Laotians, almost all civilians. Prior to this destruction, the Pathet Lao Communists controlled only one-third of the country. By 1975, Laos was ruled by a Communist government.

The destruction in Laos, though, did not end in 1973, because more than 30 percent of the bombs that were dropped during that nine-year period did not explode. Most were cluster bombs that a child could confuse for a toy; the resulting explosion sends out small projectiles meant to injure humans and destroy machines.[113] Since 1973, twenty thousand Laotians have been killed by these unexploded devices.

In 1970, President Nixon took the country by storm when he announced the invasion of Cambodia, quickly withdrawing just three months later. The indiscriminate bombing in defense of invading South Vietnamese troops completely tore Cambodia apart, driving millions from their homes. The pro-American Cambodian government which had no advance knowledge of the invasion took the blame from the peasants, who quickly flocked to the Communist Khmer Rouge. Civil war followed, and by 1975 the Khmer Rouge would become one of the bloodiest regimes in history. In the United States, four Ohio Kent State students were shot down while protesting the invasion, two students were killed at Mississippi's Jackson State College, and a third of US college campuses were temporarily closed due to student walkouts.

All of this in the name of containment; to contain the Communist bloc from landing on America's shores to stifle freedom and democracy. Yet all it did was expand the Communist stranglehold in the region, emotionally tear the United States apart, and turn its citizens away from those brave returning veterans. The father of containment, George F. Kennan, an expert on Russia and the Soviet Union, published his famous doctrine in the July 1947 issue of the *Foreign Affairs* magazine. In 1965, he appeared before the Senate Foreign Relations Committee, which was debating the issue of withdrawing from Vietnam. Kennan publicly stated: "There is every likelihood that a Communist regime in South Vietnam would follow a fairly independent political course."[114]

The domino theory—that communism would spread from one country to another—was disproved. Most nations in the region have abandoned communism or have begun to lean toward a capitalist economy. One simply must look at Vietnam, a country that is embracing capitalism and US investment; one that less than thirty years after the war ended became the 150th member of the World Trade Organization and was recognized by the United States government with full diplomatic coverage in 1991. The devastation in Vietnam, Laos, Cambodia, and on US soldiers and their families and friends was for nothing, but the reasons behind it live on.

Kennan's doctrine of containment only referred to the political and ideological threat of Russian communism, yet Truman and his Secretary of State Dean Acheson knowingly and willfully used it to begin the aggressive and militaristic Cold War, a "war" that as Kennan asserted in a 1987 issue of Foreign Affairs, did not have to consume the American public: "This, to my mind, was what was meant by the thought of 'containing communism' in 1946. . . . It is entirely clear to me that Soviet leaders do not want a war with us and are not planning to initiate one. In particular, I have never believed that they have seen it as in their interests to overrun Western Europe militarily, or that they would have launched an attack on that region generally even if the so-called nuclear deterrent had not existed."[115] But Truman and Acheson used this doctrine of containment to justify (according to which counts are used, either those of the Chinese or the UN), anywhere from 1.2 million to almost 1.6 million dead or wounded in Korea.

Almost thirty-seven thousand Americans lost their lives, and another ninety-two thousand were maimed (simply watch reruns of *MASH* to see how it played out), in a clash that wasn't even called a war—Truman and Acheson termed it "a police action." Lasting for three years, the devastation on the country and its inhabitants was enormous, with the United States continuing to have 28,500 troops stationed in South Korea, situated on over 100 bases around the country. On April 27, 2018, Kim Jong Un of North Korea met with South Korean President Moon Jae-in in the demilitarized zone separating the nations, with both leaders promising to pursue peace.

Moon will potentially visit Pyongyang, and there lies the possibility of a near-future summit with President Trump and Kim. If unification of the Korean peninsula should one day occur, it will most likely be the final demise of the doctrine of containment, unfortunately happening approximately three-quarters of a century too late.

In God We Trust

President Eisenhower signs HR7786, June 1, 1954. This ceremony changed Armistice Day to Veterans Day. The scene must have been similar when he signed three other bills from 1954 to 1956 that reinforced using God and the flag as symbols for America's men and women to follow into battle. US Government, Eisenhower Presidential Library and Museum, 1954.

Various sources in the last ten to fifteen years points to the fact that roughly 90 percent of all Americans believe in God or a universal spirit, translating to roughly 300 million Americans, including schoolchildren. If an entity wished to control its citizenry, to mold the masses to its every whim, what better method than to use God as the reason to honor the nation and lead troops into battle? The Founding Fathers intended God to watch over the first truly free nation the world had ever seen. Various subsequent administrations saw the Deity as giving America the God-given right to encroach upon sovereign people in order to expand its borders and economic reach at any cost. You're already aware that the Carnegie Foundation concluded that war was the only method to change the course of a people. Following World War II, another think tank must have come to the conclusion that, besides fear and hatred, the insertion of a Deity into America's daily life was a necessary means in controlling those same people.

In 1892, socialist Baptist minister Francis Bellamy and publishing marketing executive James B. Upham arranged in conjunction with President Benjamin Harrison to celebrate Columbus Day centered on an American flag ceremony and a salute.

The salute, in abbreviated format to today's version, slowly caught on until state after state enacted laws requiring that children recite the Pledge of Allegiance at the beginning of each school day. Where in the United States Constitution does it declare that an American citizen must declare their allegiance to a flag, let alone the country? As Supreme Court Justices Hugo Black and William Douglas concurred concerning the Pledge of Allegiance: "Words uttered under coercion are proof of loyalty to nothing but self-interest. Love of country must spring from willing hearts and free minds."[116]

But Americans didn't listen to Black and Douglas, and the pledge remained a harmless effort until the 1950s. On February 7, 1954, Presbyterian minister George M. Docherty delivered a sermon at the New York Avenue Presbyterian Church in Washington, DC. None other than President Dwight Eisenhower was sitting in the front pew, and Michigan Representative Louis Rabaut was also in attendance, subsequently placing his thoughts into the Congressional Record:

Dr. Docherty and I are not of the same Christian denomination, but I may say that in this matter he has hit the nail right on the head. You may argue from dawn to dusk about differing political, economic, and social systems, but the fundamental issue which is the unbridgeable gap between America and Communist Russia is a belief in Almighty God. From the root of atheism [*sic*] stems the evil weed of communism and its branches of materialism and political dictatorship. Unless we are willing to affirm our belief in the existence of God and His creator-creature relations to man, we drop man himself to the significance of a grain of sand . . .[117]

Rabaut, and subsequently Eisenhower, should have realized that an American is raised almost to the Heavens by the Constitution; that through the Forefathers, God instilled a freedom and a liberty and a justice to all that required no pledge to fulfill, or religious affirmation, and specifically prohibited it. But another seed had been planted decades before, and Dwight Eisenhower was the first president to get it to bear fruit. Signing a new law on June 14, 1954, Eisenhower publicly remarked: ". . . In this way we are reaffirming the transcendence of religious faith in America's heritage and future; in this way we shall constantly strengthen those spiritual weapons which forever will be our country's most powerful resource in peace and war."[118]

He referred to the placement of "under God" into the Pledge of Allegiance, already spoken by tens of millions of American children every school morning. Webster's defines "God" as: "The supernatural being conceived as the perfect and omnipotent and omniscient originator and ruler of the universe; the object of worship in monotheistic religions 2: any supernatural being worshipped as *controlling some part of the world or some aspect of life or who is the personification of a force* [syn: deity, divinity, immortal]." [Italics inserted by S. H. to add emphasis.]

Eisenhower was on a roll. He soon signed Public Law #104 on July 11, 1955, requiring all currency and coins to be inscribed with the motto "In God We Trust." He then placed into law another bill on July 30, 1956, Public Law 851, which made that same religious slogan the nation's new official motto, replacing "E Pluribus Unum." (Out of Many, One). Roughly thirty million Americans have no religious affiliations, and within this population are many who are atheist or agnostics with serious doubts concerning religious faith or God. The United States is also their country, and it's their Pledge of Allegiance as well.

"Out of Many, One" is the embodiment of the United States Constitution, plainly suggesting that from many colonies, we emerge as one; of the various races, creeds, nationalities, the United States of America is a melting pot of one nation—no matter how different we are, or where we come from, or what we believe as individuals, we are all Americans. Unfortunately, though, you can't follow "Out of Many, One" into battle.

The average American child recites the Pledge of Allegiance approximately two thousand five hundred times during their school years, and how many times in their lives will they subliminally see their coins inscribed with "In God We Trust?" The early 1950s saw a unified effort of extreme nationalism drilled into American citizens each and every day for the apparent and obvious supreme purpose of indoctrination. The country would now be more important than the individual, in direct opposition to the purpose of the United States Constitution and the Bill of Rights:

- "One nation under God" is a pledge of allegiance to a flag that can be followed into battle, rather than a pledge to the United States Constitution which guarantees individual rights and freedoms as Americans. One cannot follow a Constitution into battle.
- School children recite the pledge prior to school each and every morning.
- Girl scouts and boy scouts recite the pledge prior to every meeting.
- "The Star-Spangled Banner" is sung prior to every professional sports game. Approximately seventy-five million Major League Baseball attendees annually honor America, rather

than honoring their freedoms, rights, and democratic privileges, during every baseball game throughout each season.

Ken Lynn, an active duty Air Force officer stationed in Alabama in 1999, wrote:

When we pledge allegiance, what are we doing? According to Black's Law Dictionary, 6th edition, allegiance is defined as: "Obligation of fidelity and obedience to government in consideration for protection that government gives." Although the flag represents the embodiment of our national conscience and is easily the most recognized symbol of our nation, one that I proudly support and defend daily as a member of our nation's Armed Forces, I find it curious that a "religious" Pledge of Allegiance to our flag rather than a Pledge of Allegiance to our secular Constitution has become the institutionalized form of patriotism in our country. Members of the military are required to swear or affirm their support and defense of the Constitution of the United States. I have gladly "pledged my allegiance" by making this affirmation, and I, like many other atheists in foxholes, would give my life if necessary to defend our Constitution and our great democratic way of life.[119]

Operation Northwoods

THE JOINT CHIEFS OF STAFF
WASHINGTON 25, D.C.

UNCLASSIFIED

13 March 1962

MEMORANDUM FOR THE SECRETARY OF DEFENSE

Subject: Justification for US Military Intervention in Cuba (TS)

1. The Joint Chiefs of Staff have considered the attached Memorandum for the Chief of Operations, Cuba Project, which responds to a request of that office for brief but precise description of pretexts which would provide justification for US military intervention in Cuba.

2. The Joint Chiefs of Staff recommend that the proposed memorandum be forwarded as a preliminary submission suitable for planning purposes. It is assumed that there will be similar submissions from other agencies and that these inputs will be used as a basis for developing a time-phased plan. Individual projects can then be considered on a case-by-case basis.

3. Further, it is assumed that a single agency will be given the primary responsibility for developing military and para-military aspects of the basic plan. It is recommended that this responsibility for both overt and covert military operations be assigned the Joint Chiefs of Staff.

For the Joint Chiefs of Staff:

L. L. Lemnitzer

L. L. LEMNITZER
Chairman
Joint Chiefs of Staff

SYSTEMATICALLY REVIEWED
BY JCS ON _21 May 84_
CLASSIFICATION CONTINUED

1 Enclosure
Memo for Chief of Operations, Cuba Project

EXCLUDED FROM GDS

EXCLUDED FROM AUTOMATIC
REGRADING; DOD DIR 5200.10
DOES NOT APPLY

Operation Northwoods Memo.

In the only known existing document of its kind, the United States government, in the form of the highest-ranking officers of the US military, proposed on March 13, 1962, to commit acts of terrorism against American military personnel, military ships and bases, and American citizens. Discovered among more than 1,500 pages of unclassified documents in the late 1990s, the document was signed by General Lyman L. Lemnitzer, Chairman of the Joint Chiefs of Staff. The subject of the memo introducing the document is: "Justification for military intervention in Cuba." Here are some of the "highlights," with only a few misspelled words corrected in italics:

- It is recognized that any action which becomes pretext for US military intervention in Cuba will lead to a political decision which then would lead to military action.
- Such a plan would enable a logical build-up of incidents to be combined with other seemingly unrelated events to camouflage the ultimate objective and create the necessary impression of Cuban rashness and irresponsibility on a large scale, directed at other countries as well as the United States. . . . The desired resultant from the execution of this plan would be to place the United States in the apparent position of suffering defensible grievances from a rash and irresponsible government of Cuba and to develop an international image of a Cuban threat to peace in the Western Hemisphere.
- A series of *well-coordinated* incidents will be planned to take place in and around Guantanamo to give genuine appearance of being done by hostile Cuban forces.
  a. Incidents to establish a credible attack (not in chronological order):
  1. Start rumors (many). Use clandestine radio.
  2. Land friendly Cubans in uniform "over-the-fence" to stage attack on base.
  3. Capture Cuban (friendly) saboteurs inside the base.
  4. Start riots near the base main gate (friendly Cubans).
  5. Blow up ammunition inside the base; start fires.
  6. Burn aircraft on air base (sabotage).

7. Lob mortar shells from outside of base into base. Some damage to installations.
8. Capture assault teams approaching from the sea or vicinity of Guantanamo City.
9. Capture militia group which storms the base.
10. Sabotage ship in harbor; large fires—naphthalene.
11. Sink ship near harbor entrance. Conduct funerals for mock-victims . . .

b. United States would respond by executing offensive operations to secure water and power supplies, destroying artillery and mortar emplacements which threaten the base.

c. Commence large scale United States military operations.

• A "Remember the Maine" incident could be arranged in several forms:

a. We could blow up a US ship in Guantanamo Bay and blame Cuba. [S. H. Note: Is this an admittance by the Joint Chiefs in 1962 that US. military forces intentionally started an explosion on the USS Maine in the Cuban Harbor in 1898, causing the loss of 260 US service personnel to begin the Spanish-American War?]

b. We could blow up a drone (unmanned) vessel anywhere in the Cuban waters. We could arrange to cause such incident in the vicinity of Havana or Santiago as a spectacular result of Cuban attack from the air or sea, or both. The presence of Cuban planes or ships merely investigating the intent of the vessel could be fairly compelling evidence that the ship was taken under attack. The nearness to Havana or Santiago would add credibility especially to those people that might have heard the blast or have seen the fire. The US could follow up with an air/sea rescue operation covered by US fighters to "evacuate" remaining members of the non-existent crew. Casualty lists in US newspapers would cause a helpful wave of national indignation.

• We could develop a Communist Cuban terror campaign in the Miami area, in other Florida cities and even in Washington. . . . We could sink a boatload of Cubans enroute to Florida (real or simulated). We could foster attempts on lives of Cuban refugees in the United States even to the extent of wounding in instances to be widely publicized. Exploding a few plastic bombs in carefully chosen spots, the arrest of Cuban agents and the release of prepared documents substantiating Cuban Involvement, also would be helpful in projecting the idea of an irresponsible government.

- Use of MIG type aircraft by US pilots could provide additional provocation. . . . It is possible to create an incident which will demonstrate convincingly that a Cuban aircraft has attacked and shot down a chartered civil airliner enroute from the United States to Jamaica, Guatemala, Panama, or Venezuela. The destination would be chosen only to cause the flight plan route to cross Cuba. The passengers could be a group of college students off on a holiday or any grouping of persons with a common interest to support chartering a non-scheduled flight.

  a. An aircraft at Eglin AFB would be painted and numbered as an exact duplicate for a civil registered aircraft belonging to a CIA proprietary organization in the Miami area. At a designated time the duplicate would be substituted for the actual civil aircraft and would be loaded with the selected passengers, all boarded under carefully prepared aliases. The actual registered aircraft would be converted to a drone.

  b. Take-off times of the drone aircraft and the actual aircraft will be scheduled to allow a rendezvous south of Florida. From the rendezvous point the passenger-carrying aircraft will descend to minimum altitude and go directly into an auxiliary field at Eglin AFB where arrangements will have been made to evacuate the passengers and return the aircraft to its original status. The drone aircraft meanwhile will continue to fly the filed flight plan. When over Cuba the drone will being transmitting on the international distress frequency a "MAY DAY" message stating he is under attack by Cuban MIG aircraft. The transmission will be interrupted by destruction of the aircraft which will be triggered by radio signal. This will allow ICAO radio stations in the Western hemisphere to tell the US what has happened to the aircraft instead of the US trying to "sell" the incident.

- It is possible to create an incident which will make it appear that Communist Cuban MIGs have destroyed a USAF aircraft over International waters in an unprovoked attack.[120]

If not for President Kennedy and his Attorney General Robert F. Kennedy nixing this proposal, the United States almost certainly would have attacked and regime-removed an autonomous government in Cuba in 1962, exactly as the United States did in 2001 and 2003 when they regime-removed the Taliban in Afghanistan and Saddam Hussein in Iraq, respectively. We know for certain from this document that justification for that action would almost certainly have taken American and Cuban refugee life and limbs. The big question is whether or not the justification for American action in 2001 and 2003 came from another document justifying the loss of American life on September 11.

It should be further noted that the last entry of the Operation Northwoods document, Enclosure B, states, "It is understood that the Department of State also is preparing suggested courses of action to develop justification for US military intervention in Cuba."[121]

As will be seen next, Kennedy was distancing himself from most of the powers in Washington, and now he could add the military and the State Department to the list of branches and agencies disenchanted with its presidency. Add the CIA and the military industrial complex to this ever-growing list, and all the ingredients are present to launch the second successful coup d'état in United States history.

The Second Successful American Coup d'état:

The JFK Assassination

October 18, 1962, in the Oval Office: President Kennedy, Soviet Deputy Minister Vladimir S. Seyemenov, Ambassador of the USSR Anatoly F. Dobrynin, and Soviet Minister of Foreign Affairs Andrel Gromyko. Robert L. Knudson, US National Archives and Recordings Administration, 1962.

We are not going to delve into any of the JFK conspiracy theories, such as the magic bullet or the multiple gunmen. The grassy knoll and the mafia will be left to Jim Garrison and Oliver Stone, because it doesn't matter how many bullets or how many gunmen shot the president of the United States, or even if Lee Harvey Oswald was actually involved. The fact remains that JFK's presidential motorcade is the only procession in the history of the known world where the victim was led to the assassin—a man allegedly went to his place of work on the sixth floor of an office building, took a coffee break, and a little later allegedly went to a window on the same floor and shot and killed a world leader handed to him on a silver platter in an open motorcade.

Roughly six weeks prior to the November 22, 1963, assassination, Lee Harvey Oswald applied for a job at the Texas School Book Depository that overlooked Dealey Plaza. Three days prior on November 19, both the *Dallas Morning News* and the *Dallas Times-Herald* published the president's motorcade route from Love Field to the Trade Mart where he was to speak. Oswald presumably read one of these announcements that the man he allegedly hated enough to kill would be six floors below him in less than seventy-two hours. Lee Harvey Oswald, the only alleged assassin in the history of the world who didn't have to pursue his victim.

Conspiracy theorists waste their efforts attempting to prove whether or not Oswald fired the shots that killed JFK, or if there were multiple gunmen. They are moot points. The key is that if Oswald, alone or with other conspirators, had not succeeded in killing him, President Kennedy would never have made it to a second term anyway:

- Following the Cuban Missile Crisis, JFK and Khrushchev were in negotiations on a limited nuclear test-ban treaty that would have severely hindered the military-industrial machine. Many generals and top government officials, especially within the CIA, considered this to be an act of treason. They were preparing for escalated hostilities in Vietnam and the overthrow of Castro in Cuba, yet their president was preparing for peace. On June 10, 1963 (less than five months prior to his death), Kennedy addressed the graduating class of American University. In a powerful plea, he said, "Every thoughtful citizen who despairs of war and wishes to bring peace, should begin by looking inward. . . . War makes no sense in an age when the deadly poisons produced by a nuclear exchange would be carried by wind and water and soil and seed to the far corners of the globe and to generations yet unborn. . . ." And finally, Kennedy stated, "I am taking this opportunity, therefore, to announce two important decisions in this regard. First: Chairman Khrushchev, Prime Minister Macmillan, and I have agreed that high-level discussions will shortly begin in Moscow looking toward early agreement on a comprehensive test ban treaty. Our hopes must be tempered with the caution of history—but with our hopes go the hopes of all mankind. Second: To make clear our good faith and solemn convictions on the matter, I now declare that the United States does not propose to conduct nuclear tests in the atmosphere so long as other states do not do so. We will not be the first to resume. Such a declaration is no substitute for a formal binding treaty, but I hope it will help us achieve one. Nor would such a treaty be a substitute for disarmament, but I hope it will help us achieve it."[122]

• Just a few months later, on October 11, 1963, roughly six weeks prior to the events at Dealey Plaza, the president secretly issued NSAM 263, stating that a phased withdrawal of all United States troops was to begin with one thousand troops exiting Vietnam by the end of 1963. This decision was based on a report submitted to him on October 2 by Defense Secretary Robert McNamara and Chairman of the Joint Chiefs of Staff, General Maxwell Taylor, also specifying that all troops be withdrawn by the end of 1965.

On November 12, just ten days before his assassination, President Kennedy publicly stated at a press conference that our goals regarding South Vietnam were to bring Americans home, and to intensify the struggle. Nowhere in those remarks was one mention of victory, a turnaround from prior remarks on the subject.

Two days prior to Dealey Plaza, senior Cabinet members and military officials met in Honolulu and issued OPLAN 34A, intended for presentation to the president, which called for intensified sabotage raids against the North utilizing Vietnamese commandos under US supervision. Quite significantly, these plans were not shown to Defense Secretary McNamara, and Kennedy's withdrawal order was being sabotaged by plans to ship out soldiers who were due for rotation out of Vietnam anyway, rather than withdrawing full units. This was planned escalation by administration officials and the US military, in direct conflict with JFK's NSAM 263, two days before a new president would be sworn in.[123]

- JFK was secretly negotiating with Fidel Castro to bring peace between the two countries. Lisa Howard, actress turned newswoman, was the anchor for ABC's *The News Hour with Lisa Howard*. Upon her return from interviewing Castro in Cuba in April 1963, Howard reported back to Deputy CIA Director Richard Helms that Castro wanted to talk peace. Helms sent a memo to Kennedy saying, "Castro is ready to discuss rapprochement, and she [Howard] herself is ready to discuss it with him if asked to do so by the US Government."[124]

  CIA Director John McCone must have been totally opposed to this, and Arthur Schlesinger explained why in 1976: "The CIA was reviving the [Castro] assassination plots at the very time President Kennedy was considering the possibility of normalization of relations with Cuba—an extraordinary action. If it was not total incompetence—which in the case of the CIA cannot be excluded—it was a studied attempt to subvert national policy."[125]

  Howard bypassed the CIA, and wrote in the *War and Peace Report* journal that Castro really wanted to begin negotiations with the United States: "In our conversations he made it quite clear that he was ready to discuss: the Soviet personnel and

THE WHITE HOUSE
WASHINGTON

TOP SECRET - EYES ONLY   October 11, 1963

NATIONAL SECURITY ACTION MEMORANDUM NO. 263

TO: Secretary of State
           Secretary of Defense
           Chairman of the Joint Chiefs of Staff

SUBJECT: South Vietnam

At a meeting on October 5, 1963, the President considered the
recommendations contained in the report of Secretary McNamara
and General Taylor on their mission to South Vietnam.

The President approved the military recommendations contained
in Section I B (1-3) of the report, but directed that no formal
announcement be made of the implementation of plans to withdraw 1,000 U.S. military personnel by the end of 1963.

After discussion of the remaining recommendations of the report,
the President approved an instruction to Ambassador Lodge which
is set forth in State Department telegram No. 534 to Saigon.

                                    McGeorge Bundy

Copy furnished:
    Director of Central Intelligence
    Administrator, Agency for International Development

                                    cc:
                                        Mr. Bundy ✓
                                        Mr. Forrestal
                                        Mr. Johnson
                    TOP SECRET - EYES ONLY   NSC Files

                    DECLASSIFIED
            E. O. 11652, SEC. 3(E), 5(D), 5(5) A' 2-11

        Committee Print of Pentagon Papers
            BY HS2   NARS, DATE 7/15/77

National Security Action Memorandum No. 263. Unknown or not provided Author,
National Archives and Records Administration, October 11, 1962.

military hardware on Cuban soil; compensation for expropri-
ated American lands and investments; the question of Cuba as a
base for Communist subversion throughout the Hemisphere."
After much talk on both sides (Castro even offered to send a
plane to Mexico to pick up a Kennedy representative to iron

out last-minute details), eight days prior to the assassination, Howard sent a message to her Cuban contact that the president wished to talk.

On November 18, now three days prior to his death, JFK sent a coded message to Castro in a speech he delivered in Miami at the Inter-American Press Association: "They have made Cuba a victim of foreign imperialism, an instrument of the policy of others, a weapon in an effort dictated by external powers to subvert the other American Republics. This, and this alone, divides us. As long as this is true, nothing is possible. Without it, everything is possible."[126]

French journalist Jean Daniel, delivering a message from Kennedy, was with Castro when the news of the assassination came in. Daniel reported that Castro said, "That's the end of your peace mission. Everything is changed." President Johnson was told in December 1963 of the proposed peace talks with Castro. He refused to continue the talks. Howard continued her attempts, however, and as a result, she was fired by ABC, because she had "chosen to participate publicly in partisan political activity contrary to long-established ABC news policy."[127]

Operation Northwoods: As previously discussed, the Joint Chiefs, presumably in conjunction with the CIA and definitely in conjunction with the State Department, were prepared to fabricate a false flag military attack on the United States in order to provoke war with Cuba, and potentially the Russians. Could they really wait for JFK to complete his almost certain eight years in office?

John F. Kennedy was the first US president since Abraham Lincoln to alienate the office from the forces of the military, big business, and the money powers. He was becoming almost totally autonomous, utilizing the presidency for what he felt was for the betterment of the country. Détente with the Soviet Union and Cuba would have proven disastrous to the military-industrial complex, especially when it came time to escalate hostilities in Vietnam. A limited nuclear disarmament pact with the Soviet Union would have made the domino theory of communist containment a lot less likely for the American public to swallow, meaning potentially billions less in military spending and profits in the decades to come, and far less control for the military. These same forces must have been horrified at the prospect of a friendly Communist Cuba, especially the president negotiating peace with a leader they were trying to kill.

A coup was the only alternative. With either Vice President Lyndon Johnson's direct participation or his coercion into cooperating, the government of the United States of America changed hands immediately, with LBJ sworn in as president aboard Air Force One. Almost as soon as Johnson deplaned and entered the White House, America's war activity in Vietnam increased, and détente with Cuba and the Soviet Union ceased to exist. A perfect plot—involve a Communist-leaning and pro-Cuba activist Lee Harvey Oswald, place him six stories above an open presidential motorcade with a high-powered rifle (with additional firepower assistance or not), and swear in a puppet president to execute a 180-degree turn in Kennedy's American foreign policy.

They had destined Vietnam as the next Korean war machine, a war to test their various new weapons. They would pour the country's money into it in order to drive up the national debt and their profit, issue the huge contracts for the necessary war materials, and encroach their military bases and warplanes even further into Asia with almost total control over the Southeast portion of the continent. The wealth and strategic power would have been staggering.

President Kennedy, though, had issued orders for all American troops to be withdrawn by 1965, the year he would have almost definitely begun his second term. President Reagan is revered for his part in ending the Cold War; JFK had plans to end it more than two decades earlier and would most likely have done so if it weren't for a successful coup. Four days after his assassination, and one day after his funeral, President Lyndon Baines Johnson issued NSAM 273, approving intensified covert actions against the North Vietnamese, a preliminary draft (OPLAN 34A) of which was drawn up just two days prior to Dealey Plaza in Honolulu, Hawaii. Paragraph Seven states: "Planning should include different levels of possible increased activity, and in each instance there be estimates such factors as: A. Resulting damage to North Vietnam; B. The plausibility denial; C. Vietnamese retaliation; D. Other international reaction. Plans submitted promptly for approval by authority."

Retired US Army Major John M. Newman was an intelligence officer stationed at Fort Meade, the headquarters of the National Security Agency. James K. Galbraith discussed Newman's book *JFK and Vietnam* in the *Boston Review* and concluded, "John F. Kennedy had formally decided to withdraw from Vietnam, whether we were winning or not. Robert McNamara, who did not believe we were winning, supported this decision. The first stage of withdrawal had been ordered. The final date, two years later, had been specified. These decisions were taken, and even placed, in an oblique and carefully limited way, before the public."[128]

The point, though, is really not if JFK would have withdrawn from Vietnam completely by 1965 or would have reached détente with Russia and Cuba—significantly reducing the perception of a Red Menace—it is that the United States government, from Vice President Johnson, to the CIA and FBI, to the Cabinet, to the Joint Chiefs of Staff, the NSA, and all of his advisers *believed* that President Kennedy was heading in those directions. Short of praying for a loss at the polls in the 1964 election, their only course of action and a deterrent was a coup.

A little more than a year before his death, JFK was discussing the film *Seven Days in May* with some friends and commented, "It's possible. We could have a military takeover in this country, but the conditions would have to be just right. If, for example, we had a young president, and he had a Bay of Pigs, there would be a certain uneasiness."[129]

Just one week after the assassination, as reported by historians Timothy Naftali and Aleksandr Fursenko from declassified Soviet documents, William Walton delivered a message to Khrushchev from Attorney General Robert F. Kennedy which claimed that "domestic hard-liners, rather than foreign agents, were responsible" for JFK's murder.[130]

According to journalist Bill Moyers, then special assistant to

President Johnson, LBJ stated on November 24, 1963, one day *before* JFK was buried, "They'll think with Kennedy dead we've lost heart. . . . They'll think we're yellow and we don't mean what we say. . . . The Chinese. The fellas in the Kremlin. They'll be taking the measure of us. They'll be wondering just how far they can go. . . . I'm going to give those fellas out there the money they want. This crowd today says a hundred or so million will make the difference. . . . I told them they got it—more if they need it. I told them I'm not going to let Vietnam go the way of China. . . ."[131] LBJ had just met with, among others, Secretary of State Dean Rusk, Secretary of Defense Robert McNamara, George Ball, McGeorge Bundy, Ambassador to South Vietnam Henry Cabot Lodge, and CIA Director McCone. Two days later, Johnson signed NSAM 273.

The CIA and the Pentagon openly preached for war with North Vietnam, the overthrow of Castro, and a build-up of our military and nuclear arsenal. With the exception of a few loners, President Kennedy was proceeding on a collision course with almost the entire Washington establishment. From the June 10, 1963, commencement speech at American University, to NSAM 263, to his potentially favorable conversations with Castro, JFK's "treasonous actions" had to be silenced, eradicated, and his policies reversed. A simple assassination would have been completely ineffective if LBJ had not cooperated; and by his actions concerning Vietnam, Cuba, and the Soviets, he certainly did from the moment he took the oath of office. Could the mafia have gotten to LBJ? Castro? The Russians? Could any of them have delivered the president to Oswald and/or other gunmen on the grassy knoll in an open motorcade? Only the CIA, FBI, Secret Service, and/or the Pentagon had the power, and the immediate need, to pull it off.

Kennedy was after peace. It would become his legacy. But the real power in the country lay in the military and the CIA, and they effectively totally changed American history in the latter part of the twentieth century. As Peter Janney writes in *Mary's Mosaic*:

They had killed Jack because he and his ally-in-peace Nikita Khrushchev were steering the world away from the Cold War toward peace, thereby eliminating the military-industrial-intelligence complex's most treasured weapons—the fear of war, the fear of "Communist takeover," and the manipulative use of Fear itself. The Cold War was about to end, and with it the covert action arm of the Central Intelligence Agency. The Agency would have been all but neutered, its funding and resources cut, its menacing grip on public opinion exposed and eliminated. It also meant the eventual curtailment of many of the defense industries, including the proliferation of nuclear arms. There would have been no war in Southeast Asia or Vietnam; that, too, was about to end. A rapprochement with Fidel Castro and Cuba was on the horizon. Both Jack and Fidel wanted "a lasting peace."

Simply put, peace—particularly world peace—wasn't good for business, nor for American military and economic hegemony. Whatever enlightenment Mary and Jack may have finally engendered together, it had evolved into a part of Jack's newfound trajectory of where he wanted to take not only his presidency in 1963, but the entire world. It was the pursuit of peace that was about to take center stage. . . .[132]

One day prior to Dealey Square, JFK read the latest Vietnam casualty report stating that 100 Americans had died so far and commented to his Assistant Press Secretary Malcolm Kilduff: "It's time for us to get out. . . . After I come back from Texas, that's going to change. There's no reason for us to lose another man over there. Vietnam is not worth another American life."[133] Within twelve years of the illegal seizure of the United States government on November 22, 1963, 58,120 more US servicemen and women perished, 304,000 were wounded, and millions of Vietnamese, Laotians, and Cambodians were killed, wounded, and displaced from their homes.

1964: The Gulf of Tonkin Deception

President Lyndon B. Johnson signs the Gulf of Tonkin Resolution, White House East Room, August 1964. Cecil W. Stoughton, National Archives and Record Administration, August 10, 1964.

On August 2, 1964, the USS *Maddox* and the USS *Turner Joy* were patrolling in international waters in the Gulf of Tonkin and were presumably approached by North Vietnamese gunboats. The gunboats opened fire on the *Maddox*, and a lengthy battle ensued. The United States then retaliated with air attacks on North Vietnam. On August 4, 1964, the United States again claimed that the North Vietnamese engaged them in battle, prompting Congress to adopt the Gulf of Tonkin Resolution. Passed on August 7, 1964, and adopted three days later on August 10, it effectively authorized the president, without any declaration of war, to do whatever was necessary in order to assist any member or protocol state of the Southeast Asia Collective Defense Treaty, which included involving armed forces.

Later research indicated that the attacks did not actually occur. Daniel Ellsberg, who released the *Pentagon Papers*, has stated that he deeply regretted keeping silent for so long, feeling that he might have been part of a governmental conspiracy to get the United States into a war. CBS News Political analyst Leonard Steinhorn, professor of Communication and affiliate professor of history at American University, had this to say on August 4, 2014, in the *Huffington Post*:

> Fifty years ago, on August 10, 1964, President Lyndon Johnson signed what is known as the Gulf of Tonkin Resolution. It is a day that should live in infamy. . . . History has shown that the resolution was built on a foundation of misinformation, fabrication, and willful evasion of the truth. Contrary to what the president claimed, there was no unprovoked "act of aggression" against the American destroyers that were patrolling the Tonkin Gulf, and a second alleged incident never even took place. By the time Lyndon Johnson left office more than four years later, we had amassed over half a million troops in Vietnam, lost nearly thirty-seven thousand soldiers, dropped more bomb tonnage than we had in all of World War II, released chemical weapons—Napalm and Agent Orange—throughout Southeast Asia, and burned thousands of South Vietnamese homes and villages to the ground. . . .

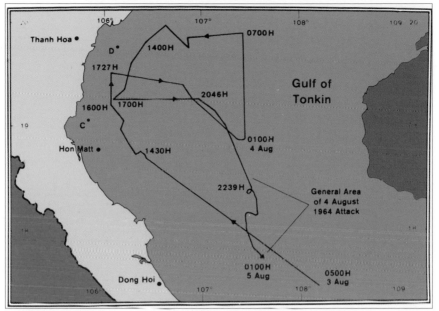

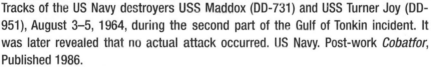

Tracks of the US Navy destroyers USS Maddox (DD-731) and USS Turner Joy (DD-951), August 3–5, 1964, during the second part of the Gulf of Tonkin incident. It was later revealed that no actual attack occurred. US Navy. Post-work *Cobatfor*, Published 1986.

Years later Senator Wayne Morse of Oregon, one of two who voted against the Gulf of Tonkin Resolution, told Ellsberg that if members of Congress had seen the evidence from the Pentagon Papers in 1964, the Tonkin Gulf Resolution would never have gotten out of committee, and if it had been brought to the floor, it would have been voted down.

What Lyndon Johnson saw as a ploy to grant him war powers ended up harming so many and transforming our nation in ways the president surely never intended. It would end up engulfing the liberalism he so loved. The Gulf of Tonkin Resolution and the hubris behind it were the linchpins of Johnson's Shakespearean Vietnam tragedy—and ours as well.[134]

With JFK out of the way for just less than a year, LBJ and his administration fabricated an excuse to pour US soldiers and war machinery into Vietnam and got the required permission from Congress.

The Assassinations of MLK and RFK:

The Third Successful Coup d'état

in American History

Attorney General Kennedy and Rev. Dr. Martin Luther King Jr., June 22, 1963, Washington, DC, Abbie Rowe, National Park Service, John Fitzgerald Kennedy Library.

Barely two months apart, and just a few months prior to the Democratic National Convention to select a presidential candidate to run against Richard M. Nixon, the two most vocal and prominent Americans against the Vietnam War were eliminated. The two people who would have campaigned vigorously against Nixon and the continuation of the war, with a huge and vibrant following, were presumably assassinated by wackos—a Palestinian who hated Robert F. Kennedy's pro-Israel stance, and a petty-thief racist who wanted to eliminate arguably the most prominent African American on the face of the earth.

In addition to the continuation of the Vietnam War, corporate America and the money powers were primed to remove the last remnant of the gold standard. Richard Nixon was their targeted puppet to take care of business, which he obligingly did in 1971, two years after taking office, with what the press coined as the "Nixon Shock." An independent RFK, like his assassinated brother, would almost certainly never have agreed to this.

Though Hubert Humphrey was ahead of Kennedy in the delegate count needed for nomination at the time of RFK's assassination, Kennedy was confident that he would garner the necessary votes at the convention. Regardless, with Kennedy and King campaigning for Humphrey, the Democratic party would have been much more unified, with a much better chance to overcome the November 1968 Nixon election plurality of a half million popular votes and the loss of nineteen states. But lady luck can only go so far. Once again, the devastation of the Vietnam War would be allowed to escalate, with the violence continuing for another seven years, with the country's (and the world's) economy ripe for what would occur over the next few decades with the gold standard out of the way.

Though insiders have known for a half century, J. Edgar Hoover's hatred for Martin Luther King has only relatively recently been brought to the public attention. In November 1964, Hoover had characterized King as the most notorious liar in the country.[135] The National Archives, in the "JFK Assassination Records, Findings On MLK Assassination" collection, states that having found no governmental agency was involved in the assassination of King (as in the case of the Warren Commission), the committee was concerned with the Department of Justice and the FBI, since the Bureau had conducted an active campaign to discredit King and to compromise his standing in society. Just a few of the startling revelations contained in this report:

- "Hoover's irritation resulted in a sharp and immediate change in the position of the Domestic Intelligence Division. Reacting to Dr. King's famous 'I Have a Dream' address, FBI Assistant Director Sullivan wrote in a memorandum to Assistant to the Director Alan Belmont:

  'The Director is correct. We were completely wrong about believing the evidence was not sufficient to determine some years ago that Fidel Castro was not a Communist or under Communist influence. In investigating and writing about communists and the American Negro, we had better remember this and profit by the lesson it should teach.

  . . . Personally, I believe in the light of King's powerful demagogic speech yesterday he stands head and shoulders over all other Negro leaders put together when it comes to influencing great masses of Negroes. We must mark him now, if we have not done so before, as the most dangerous Negro of the future in this Nation from the standpoint of communist, the Negro, and national security.'

- By the end of 1963, FBI files reflected a marked difference in the Bureau's approach toward King and the beginning of a campaign to discredit him. On December 23, 1963, a conference was held in Washington with members of the Atlanta field office and the headquarters Domestic Intelligence Division in attendance. A memorandum written by Sullivan the following day summarized the results of the meeting:

  'Recognizing the delicacy of this entire situation because of the prominence of King, the primary purpose of the conference was to explore how best to carry on one investigation to produce the desired results without embarrassment to the Bureau. Included in the discussion was a complete analysis of the avenues of approach aimed at neutralizing King as an effective Negro leader and developing evidence concerning King's continued dependence on Communists, for guidance and direction.'

- Less than two weeks later, the direction of the Bureau's developing course of action became clear. Assistant Director Sullivan authorized a proposal that the FBI consider promoting a new leader for the Black community who would alleviate the confusion expected once King had been 'taken off his pedestal.' Hoover attached a note to Sullivan's memo:

   'I am glad to see that light has finally, though dismally delayed, come to the DID (Domestic Intelligence Division). I struggled for months to get over the fact that the Communists were taking over the racial movement but our experts here couldn't and wouldn't see it.'[136]

Civil Rights march on Washington. Rowland Scherman, August 28, 1963.

The FBI's "Mission and Priorities" page on its website states its core values as, "Uncompromising personal integrity of all those we protect . . . Accountability for accepting responsibility for our actions . . . Diversity." So in 1963, a full five years prior to MLK's assassination, America's federal and centralized police agency, marked King and discussed ways to neutralize a leader of the black community.

Sirhan B. Sirhan and Chappaquiddick completed the eradication of arguably the most prominent political family of its time, one which besides its womanizing tendencies, generally believed in progressive social and economic change, and was not afraid to independently exert and espouse its beliefs. Sirhan claims that he killed Robert F. Kennedy to bring the world's attention to the plight of Palestine, and innocent bystander Mary Jo Kopechne died when Ted Kennedy drove their car over a bridge. Barely kept out of jail, any chance Ted had for a White House run was effectively ruined. In just over a decade, the Kennedys were politically destroyed on the national platform.

Effectively, as was the case on November 22, 1963, the elimination of MLK and RFK proved to be a successful coup d'état. As soon as Kennedy was pronounced dead on June 6, 1968, with MLK already deceased, the election of Richard M. Nixon was virtually assured. Almost immediately, in the span of fewer than two months, the national political landscape was illegally changed by force.

MARTIN LUTHER KING: April 4, 1968

The Reverend Martin Luther King Jr. was getting more and more powerful, not only within the black community but with white liberals as well. James Earl Ray allegedly shot King with a Remington rifle, presumably from the bathroom window of a flophouse across the street from King's hotel, firing a single shot through his head. There were no witnesses to the actual shooting, but someone claimed they saw a man leaving the bathroom at around the same time, and another saw a male run to a white Mustang and drive off. A bag with a rifle bearing Ray's fingerprints was found outside a nearby store.

Lee Harvey Oswald leaves a rifle on the sixth floor of the Texas

Book Depository bearing his fingerprints. Muhammad Atta takes down the World Trade Center towers in a hijacked plane but somehow miraculously leaves his passport on the ground below, and his suitcase is left behind in Boston. It contains maps and other terrorist paraphernalia. Sirhan B. Sirhan conveniently carries an anti-Robert F. Kennedy newspaper article in his shirt pocket as he's wrestled to the ground after allegedly killing Robert F. Kennedy. Petty criminal James Earl Ray manages to elude the Memphis police, leaving the country with perfectly forged documents and passports. He remains at-large for two months, unluckily being picked from a security checkpoint at Heathrow Airport in England because the alias on his passport just happened to be included on a Royal Canadian watch list.

If the security guard had not noticed this, Ray presumably could have gone free for a lifetime. Yet what did he allegedly do? What did this man who had the wits, the skill, and apparently a heck of a lot of money to pull off this nearly perfect crime, do? Instead of taking the rifle into the Mustang with him, and ditching it afterward, or at least quickly wiping it clean, he left his identity behind. The man who allegedly stalked and killed the nation's most powerful and influential civil rights leader, and eluded the police for two months when he easily could have gotten away scot-free, left behind his fingerprints and engraved prison ID on his radio, not only for his identity to be immediately known, but also to make his conviction if caught almost a certainty.

Rather than face the death penalty, James Earl Ray did the smart thing, confessing in court to the crime. He was sentenced to life, recanting that confession just three days later. There are several problems with the official story:

- Ray was not a trained sniper. There is no evidence that he even knew how to properly use a rifle with sniper capabilities.
- The bullet that killed King was never matched to Ray's rifle.
- According to Ray, a man by the name of Raul asked him to buy the rifle.

Raul is where it gets quite interesting, as will be seen from the 1999 Memphis civil trial of the King family vs. Loyd Jowers and other unknown co-conspirators. According to the findings of the Memphis jury, Martin Luther King Jr. was assassinated by a conspiracy that included agencies of the United States government. What is possibly even more startling than that conclusion is that no major news venue covered the trial; as a matter of fact, the courtroom was virtually empty. Game five of the 1994 NBA Finals was interrupted on national television for a slow-speed chase of O. J. Simpson down a Los Angeles freeway, and the world was glued to the TV for his trial and eventual not guilty verdict, yet just a few years later most Americans were not even aware that a trial was going on involving the assassination of one of the most important Americans of the twentieth century, including its conspiratorial overtones and final verdict.

Freedom of the Press is one thing; freedom of the American people to be exposed to all the news is another. As James W. Douglass says in *The King Conspiracy Exposed in Memphis*:

> I can hardly believe the fact that, apart from the courtroom participants, only Memphis TV reporter Wendell Stacy and I attended from beginning to end this historic three-and-one-half week trial. Because of journalistic neglect, scarcely anyone else in this land of ours even knows what went on in it. [. . .] [S. H. Note: Bracketed ellipses are not part of original quote.]
>
> What I experienced in that courtroom ranged from inspiration at the courage of the Kings, their lawyer-investigator William F. Pepper, and the witnesses, to amazement at the government's carefully interwoven plot to kill Dr. King. The seriousness with which US intelligence agencies planned the murder of Martin Luther King Jr. speaks eloquently of the threat Kingian nonviolence represented to the powers that be in the spring of 1968.
>
> [. . .] As soon became evident in court, the real defendants were the anonymous co-conspirators who stood in the shadows behind Jowers, the former owner of a Memphis bar and grill. The Kings and Pepper were in effect charging US intelligence agencies—particularly the FBI and Army intelligence—with organizing, subcontracting, and covering up the assassination. Such a charge guarantees almost insuperable obstacles to its

being argued in a court within the United States. Judicially, it is an unwelcome beast.

Many qualifiers have been attached to the verdict in the King case. It came not in criminal court but in civil court, where the standards of evidence are much lower than in criminal court. (For example, the plaintiffs used unsworn testimony made on audiotapes and videotapes.) Furthermore, the King family as plaintiffs and Jowers as defendant agreed ahead of time on much of the evidence.

But these observations are not entirely to the point. Because of the government's "sovereign immunity," it is not possible to put a US intelligence agency in the dock of a US criminal court. [. . .] In the end, twelve jurors, six black and six white, said to everyone willing to hear: guilty as charged . . .

[. . .] In 1993 [. . .] Jowers had gone public [. . .] to Sam Donaldson on *Prime Time Live.* He said he had been asked to help in the murder of King and was told there would be a decoy (Ray) in the plot. He was also told that the police "wouldn't be there that night."

In that interview, the transcript of which was read to the jury in the Memphis courtroom, Jowers said the man who asked him to help in the murder was a Mafia-connected produce dealer named Frank Liberto. Liberto, now deceased, had a courier deliver $100,000 for Jowers to hold at his restaurant, Jim's Grill, the back door of which opened onto the dense bushes across from the Lorraine Motel. Jowers said he was visited the day before the murder by a man named Raul, who brought a rifle in a box. [. . .]

Café owner Lavada Addison, a friend of Liberto's in the late 1970s, testified that Liberto had told her he "had Martin Luther King killed." Addison's son, Nathan Whitlock, said when he learned of this conversation he asked Liberto point-blank if he had killed King. "[Liberto] said, 'I didn't kill the nigger but I had it done.' I said, 'What about that other son-of-a-bitch taking credit for it?' He says, 'Ahh, he wasn't nothing but a trouble-maker from Missouri. He was a front man . . . a setup man.'"

[. . .] Jowers says that meetings to plan the assassination

occurred at Jim's Grill. He said planners included undercover Memphis Police Department officer Marrell McCollough (who now works for the Central Intelligence Agency [. . .]), MPD [Memphis Police Department] Lieutenant Earl Clark (who died in 1987), a third police officer, and two men Jowers did not know but thought were federal agents. [. . .]

Maynard Stiles, who in 1968 was a senior official in the Memphis Sanitation Department, confirmed in his testimony that the bushes near the rooming house were cut down. At about 7:00 a.m. on April 5, Stiles told the jury, he received a call from MPD Inspector Sam Evans "requesting assistance in clearing brush and debris from a vacant lot in the vicinity of the assassination." [. . .] "They went to that site, and under the direction of the police department, whoever was in charge there, proceeded with the clean-up in a slow, methodical, meticulous manner." [. . .]

Within hours of King's assassination, the crime scene that witnesses were identifying to the Memphis police as a cover for the shooter had been sanitized by orders of the police.

Judge Joe Brown, who had presided over two years of hearings on the rifle, testified that "67 percent of the bullets from my tests did not match the Ray rifle." He added that the unfired bullets found wrapped with it in a blanket were metallurgically different from the bullet taken from King's body, and therefore were from a different lot of ammunition. And because the rifle's scope had not been sighted, Brown said, "This weapon literally could not have hit the broadside of a barn." Holding up the 30.06 Remington 760 Gamemaster rifle, Judge Brown told the jury, "It is my opinion that this is not the murder weapon." [. . .]

Testimony which juror David Morphy later described as "awesome" was that of former CIA operative Jack Terrell, a whistle-blower in the Iran-Contra scandal. Terrell, who was dying of liver cancer in Florida, testified by videotape that his close friend J. D. Hill had confessed to him that he had been a member of an Army sniper team in Memphis assigned to shoot "an unknown target" on April 4. After training for a triangular shooting, the snipers were on their way into Memphis to take up positions in a water tower and two buildings when their mission was suddenly cancelled. Hill said he realized, when he learned of King's assassination the next day, that the team must have been part of a contingency plan to kill King if another shooter failed. [. . .]

The jury returned with a verdict after two and one-half hours. Judge James E. Swearengen of Shelby County Circuit Court, a gentle African-American man in his last few days before retirement, read the verdict aloud. The courtroom was now crowded with spectators, almost all black.

"In answer to the question, 'Did Loyd Jowers participate in a conspiracy to do harm to Dr. Martin Luther King?' your answer is 'Yes.'" The man on my left leaned forward and whispered softly, "Thank you, Jesus."

The judge continued: "Do you also find that others, including governmental agencies, were parties to this conspiracy as alleged by the defendant? Your answer to that one is also 'Yes.'" An even more heartfelt whisper: "Thank you, Jesus!"[137]

James Earl Ray was definitely part of the plot but was set up as the fall guy, not by the mafia, not by white supremacists, but—according to a jury of twelve men and women—by agencies of the United States Government. Less than two months later, Robert F. Kennedy would be next, completing a second successful coup d'état in less than five years.

ROBERT F. KENNEDY: June 6, 1968

Most of us know the story. Sirhan B. Sirhan confronted Robert F. Kennedy in the kitchen of the Ambassador Hotel. According to every observer present, Sirhan was roughly one and a half to three feet *in front* of RFK when he fired eight shots, sending Kennedy critically injured to the floor. There's only one problem with this scenario. The popular senator—the probable Democratic Party nominee for president who might just have won, bringing JFK's peaceful principles with a Vietnam exit strategy back to the White House—was shot three times, with all three bullets entering from the *rear* of his body at point-blank range. The fatal wound behind his right ear had powder burns, indicating the weapon was fired from the rear at a distance of direct contact to no more than one inch. Sirhan, according to every eyewitness, was in front of Kennedy and not close enough to have inflicted powder burns with a firearm.

And if anyone doubts collusion because it's impossible to keep so many implicated people quiet, the entire Sirhan defense team and the prosecution all knew this fact, because it is included in L.A. Coroner Thomas Noguchi's autopsy report, as follows: [138]

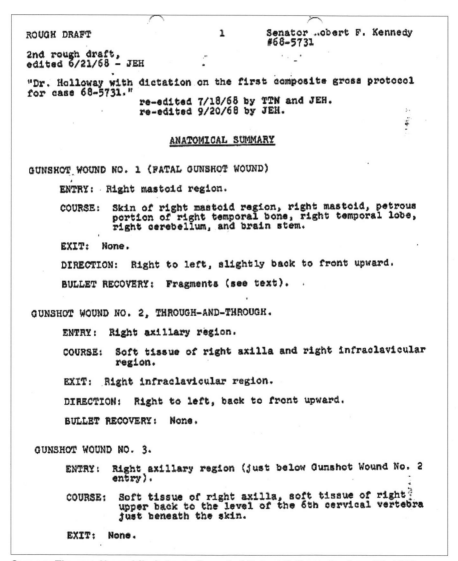

```
ROUGH DRAFT                     1        Senator ..obert F. Kennedy
                                            #68-5731
2nd rough draft,
edited 6/21/68 - JEH

"Dr. Holloway with dictation on the first composite gross protocol
for case 68-5731."
                        re-edited 7/18/68 by TTN and JEH.
                        re-edited 9/20/68 by JEH.


                        ANATOMICAL SUMMARY

GUNSHOT WOUND NO. 1 (FATAL GUNSHOT WOUND)

      ENTRY:  Right mastoid region.

      COURSE:  Skin of right mastoid region, right mastoid, petrous
               portion of right temporal bone, right temporal lobe,
               right cerebellum, and brain stem.

      EXIT:  None.

      DIRECTION:  Right to left, slightly back to front upward.

      BULLET RECOVERY:  Fragments (see text).


GUNSHOT WOUND NO. 2, THROUGH-AND-THROUGH.

      ENTRY:  Right axillary region.

      COURSE:  Soft tissue of right axilla and right infraclavicular
               region.

      EXIT:  Right infraclavicular region.

      DIRECTION:  Right to left, back to front upward.

      BULLET RECOVERY:  None.


GUNSHOT WOUND NO. 3.

      ENTRY:  Right axillary region (just below Gunshot Wound No. 2
              entry).

      COURSE:  Soft tissue of right axilla, soft tissue of right
               upper back to the level of the 6th cervical vertebra
               just beneath the skin.

      EXIT:  None.
```

Coroner Thomas Noguchi's Autopsy Report of Robert F. Kennedy, June 21, 1968.

This is page four of the medicolegal investigation signed by

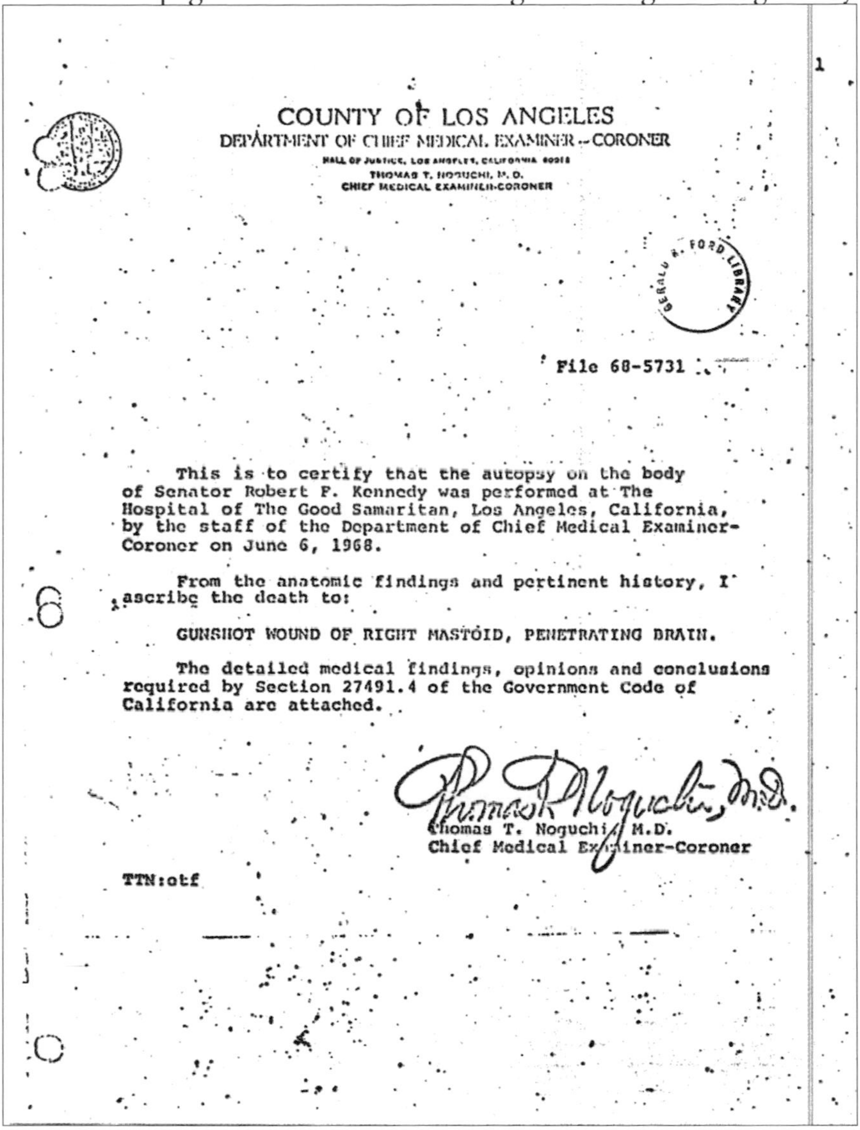

COUNTY OF LOS ANGELES
DEPARTMENT OF CHIEF MEDICAL EXAMINER — CORONER
HALL OF JUSTICE, LOS ANGELES, CALIFORNIA 90012
THOMAS T. NOGUCHI, M. D.
CHIEF MEDICAL EXAMINER-CORONER

File 68-5731

This is to certify that the autopsy on the body of Senator Robert F. Kennedy was performed at The Hospital of The Good Samaritan, Los Angeles, California, by the staff of the Department of Chief Medical Examiner-Coroner on June 6, 1968.

From the anatomic findings and pertinent history, I ascribe the death to:

GUNSHOT WOUND OF RIGHT MASTOID, PENETRATING BRAIN.

The detailed medical findings, opinions and conclusions required by Section 27491.4 of the Government Code of California are attached.

Thomas T. Noguchi, M.D.
Chief Medical Examiner-Coroner

TTN:otf

Thomas Noguchi's Medicolegal letter, Page 4.

Noguchi, showing that the cause of death is a gunshot wound to the right mastoid, which is the bone behind the right ear.[139]

The state presumably knowingly and willingly prosecuted a man for murder, when they knew from the autopsy report that the defendant, though apparently guilty of the attempted murder of the five victims that he wounded, was completely innocent of the charges of the murder of Senator Kennedy. They had to know that it was impossible for anyone to shoot a man at point-blank range in an upward trajectory from the rear when the alleged shooter was always in front of the victim and not close enough to cause powder burns. They not only prosecuted but obtained a guilty verdict with a death sentence.

Neither the FBI nor the LAPD reportedly conducted ballistic testing of the bullets found at the Ambassador Hotel. None of the three bullets that struck Kennedy were ever matched to Sirhan's gun. The prosecution, whose duty it is to protect society by convicting those responsible for crimes, never looked for a second shooter, knowing full well that Sirhan was in front of Kennedy when the three shots were fired from behind the senator.

Noguchi's autopsy report states that the fatal bullet was shot at point-blank range, entering at the rear of RFK's right ear in an upward trajectory, shattering his brain and an important artery. Again, every eyewitness placed Sirhan *in front of RFK*.

- The other two bullets hitting Kennedy all entered through his back, again in an upward trajectory.
- Sirhan's gun fired a maximum of eight shells. Between the number of bullet holes found and analysis of a sound recording made in the kitchen that night, it appears that thirteen rounds were fired.
- Major news outlets such as CNN, *Vanity Fair*, and others recently reported that Nina Rhodes-Hughes, who was one of those intimates accompanying RFK through the kitchen, reported right after the shooting to the LAPD that there were twelve to fourteen shots fired. The official LAPD archives show that she said eight.
- The LAPD's files were released twenty years after the investigation was completed and revealed that all the second shooter evidence had been either ignored or actively countered.

    Many witnesses reported seeing bullet holes in the kitchen door frames, which would have been evidence of more than eight bullets being fired.

Sirhan recently came up for parole, and in February 2016 was denied for the fifteenth time. For the first time, though, Paul Schrade—who almost died from one of Sirhan's bullets—came to his defense during the hearing and said that he should have done this a long time ago. Here is a portion of Schrade's plea for Sirhan's release:

> Sirhan, I forgive you. The evidence clearly shows you were not the gunman who shot Robert Kennedy. There is clear evidence of a second gunman in that kitchen pantry who shot Robert Kennedy. One of the bullets—the fatal bullet—struck Bob in the back of the head. Two bullets struck Bob literally in his back. A fourth bullet struck the back of his coat's upper right seam and passed harmlessly through his coat. I believe all four of those bullets were fired from a second gunman standing behind Bob. You were never behind Bob, nor was Bob's back ever exposed to you. . . .
>
> Obviously there was someone else there in that pantry also firing a gun. While Sirhan was standing in front of Bob Kennedy and his shots were creating a distraction, the other shooter secretly fired at the senator from behind and fatally wounded him. . . .
>
> First, I want to show you this. It's a letter written in 2012 by my good friend, Robert F. Kennedy Junior. Bobby wrote this letter to Eric Holder, who was then the Attorney General of the United States. In his letter to Mr. Holder, Bobby requests that federal authorities examine the Pruszynski Recording, the only known audio recording made of his father's assassination at the Ambassador Hotel. The recording was uncovered in 2004 at the California State Archives by CNN International senior writer Brad Johnson.
>
> This next document is a federal court declaration from audio expert Philip Van Praag, who Johnson recruited to analyze the Pruszynski Recording. In this document, Van Praag declares that his analysis of the recording concludes that two guns were fired in the Robert Kennedy shooting. Van Praag found a total of 13 gunshots in the Pruszynski Recording. Sirhan's one and only gun at the crime scene held no more than eight bullets and Sirhan had no opportunity to reload it. Van Praag also found

what he calls "double-shots"—meaning two gunshots fired so close together that they could not both have come from Sirhan's Iver Johnson Cadet revolver. Van Praag actually found two sets of these "double-shots."

Additionally, he found that five of the 13 gunshots featured a unique audio resonance characteristic that could not have been produced by Sirhan's gun model, meaning those five shots were fired from a second gun of a different make. . . .

These documents are statements from two witnesses to the Robert Kennedy shooting, both of them assistant maître d's for the Ambassador Hotel. These two men, Karl Uecker and Edward Minasian, escorted Robert Kennedy into the kitchen pantry immediately after the Senator delivered his victory speech in a hotel ballroom for having won the California Primary. Both Uecker and Minasian say Sirhan was in front of Bob Kennedy as the Senator walked toward Sirhan, meaning that Bob and Sirhan were facing each other. Both witnesses say Sirhan was still in front of Bob as Sirhan fired his gun. And both say that after Sirhan fired his first two shots, Uecker quickly pushed Sirhan against a steam table, placing Sirhan in a headlock while grabbing hold of Sirhan's firing arm, forcing the tip of Sirhan's gun to point away from where Bob Kennedy was and causing Sirhan to blindly fire his remaining six bullets.

In other words, Sirhan only had full control of his gun at the beginning, when he fired his first two shots, one of which hit me. Sirhan had no opportunity to fire four precisely-placed, point-blank bullets into the back of Bob Kennedy's head or body while he was pinned against that steam table and while he and Bob were facing each other. . . .

These are documents from the Los Angeles Police Department that reveal LAPD misconduct in the police investigation of the Robert Kennedy murder. They detail evidence that was destroyed while Sirhan's appeal was still pending as well as a photograph that was acknowledged by the LAPD to be "effective rebuttal" but was withheld from the defense team.

Indeed, the LAPD and L.A. County District Attorney knew two hours after the shooting of Senator Kennedy that he was shot by a second gunman and they had conclusive evidence that Sirhan could not—and did not—do it. The official record shows that the prosecution at Sirhan's trial never had one witness—and had no physical nor ballistic evidence—to prove Sirhan shot Bob Kennedy. Evidence locked up for 20 years shows that the LAPD destroyed physical evidence and hid ballistic evidence exonerating Sirhan—and covered up conclusive evidence that a second gunman fatally wounded Robert Kennedy. . . .[140]

In the end, Sirhan was turned down because he did not show remorse or understand the enormity of his crime. So if it wasn't Sirhan, then who killed Robert F. Kennedy?

Well, we'll probably never know for sure, but there was one person in the Ambassador Hotel who apparently had the means, simply because he was the only known person with Kennedy who had a gun and was close enough to inflict point-blank wounds from behind. Private security guard Thane Eugene Cesar along with maître d' Karl Uecker and a host of other people (including Nina Rhodes-Hughes and Paul Schrade) were escorting Senator Kennedy toward the Colonial Press room through the kitchen.

Cesar reportedly held Kennedy's arm with his left hand.[141]

Several years after the shooting, Cesar took a lie detector test conducted by an expert and passed it with flying colors, but it is common knowledge that people can be trained to beat the test. Though Cesar owned a .22 caliber handgun (the same caliber as Sirhan's, and the same caliber bullet taken from Kennedy's body), he claimed he sold it a few months prior to the assassination and was carrying a .38 at the time of the shooting. But an investigator proved that Cesar had sold the .22 three months *after* the shooting. Furthermore, the LAPD neither confiscated nor checked Cesar's gun at the scene of the crime, even though it was the only known weapon besides Sirhan's!

Despite all that is known today, the state of California refuses to grant Sirhan a new trial based on this evidence and is keeping a potentially innocent man in prison without a new trial, still covering up a conspiracy almost a half century later, even with mounting evidence against his conviction.

In early 1966, Robert F. Kennedy became quite outspoken about Vietnam. In his last speech to the Senate on Vietnam, Kennedy said, "Are we like the God of the Old Testament that we can decide, in Washington, DC, what cities, what towns, what hamlets in Vietnam are going to be destroyed? . . . Do we have to accept that? . . . I do not think we have to. I think we can do something about it."[142]

Less than two months before the assassination, Kennedy visited San Fernando Valley State College and addressed twelve thousand students. Taking questions afterward, he was asked who killed John Kennedy, whereupon someone else yelled, "Open the archives!" After a sigh, Kennedy responded, "I haven't answered this question before, but there would be nobody that would be more interested in all of these matters as to who was responsible for the, ah, the death of President Kennedy than I would." And to the specific question about whether he would open the Warren Commission archives, Bobby said that, if it were in his power, yes, he would, "at the appropriate time."

"Frank Mankiewicz, who as Bobby's press secretary was forever at his side, was stunned . . . Mankiewicz took it to mean that his boss would open up the investigation files if he was elected president. . . . The press secretary figured that Bobby had determined he could get to the bottom of his brother's murder only after he had regained the full reins of federal power."[143]

Using the same line of reasoning we used for JFK's demise, it doesn't matter if the same powers that killed and covered up the JFK assassination believed that RFK would reopen the investigation; no, the point is that the entire United States government, from the CIA and FBI, to the Cabinet, to the Joint Chiefs of Staff, the NSA, and all of the president's advisers *believed* that RFK would put the full thrust of the presidency behind reopening the investigation. Their only deterrent would have been to silence Bobby.

The Democratic Convention was a few short weeks away. The nominee would almost certainly be Hubert Humphrey or Robert Kennedy, with peace candidate Eugene McCarthy and Martin Luther King rallying their forces behind either RFK or Humphrey. This was a coalition that would almost certainly have been victorious against Republican nominee Richard M. Nixon, and would almost certainly have put an end to the Vietnam War which subsequently raged for another seven years. Sixteen years of Kennedy politics (assuming Teddy followed Bobby) would have been unacceptable.

Without the cohesive Democratic party that would have existed if Robert Kennedy and Martin Luther King were alive and well, Nixon won the popular vote by a half-million votes. Eugene McCarthy didn't even lend his support to eventual nominee Humphrey until a week prior to the election, even though he had a very large following in California, New Jersey, and a few other states. If McCarthy had campaigned early enough, there is a very good chance he could have rallied the electorate toward a Humphrey victory.

A coup d'état—a quick and decisive seizure of governmental power by a strong military or political group occurred between April 4 and June 6, 1968, a mere sixty-three days. A strong military and political group effectively seized governmental power for Richard M. Nixon. It's been a half century since RFK's assassination, and it has been covered up by probably two generations. The FBI and LAPD were controlled to perfection, and the media reported the official story exactly as intended.

The Stock Market Casino:

A Bubble Waiting to Happen

L ate in 2011, due to the eurozone financial crisis, the global stock markets lost a little more than $6.3 trillion![144] Ask yourself something. By and large, companies didn't lose their assets, so where did that $6.3 trillion go? Did Michele from Marseilles, or Dominick from Sicily, or your Uncle Will from Austin sell portions of their portfolio for a profit?

"Investors were more optimistic at the start of the year," said Navtej Nandra, the international head of Morgan Stanley's asset management arm, reported by the *Financial Times*.[145] There's that one word that is the key to the stock market—investors. With the exception of day traders, the average worker/investor places a small portion of his or her weekly salary into a retirement 401K, hoping to get 5, 10, or 15 percent growth in any given year, creating some funding for their golden years. Conversely, the wealthy invest for income, profit, wealth, and power, controlling the stock market with an inconceivable amount of money. That $6.3 trillion erased from the global markets didn't just disappear, most of those companies and banks didn't go under. A majority of that $6.3 trillion went right into the pockets of the wealthy around the world, presumably primarily by investors in Asian stocks where the markets dropped by a whopping 20 percent!

You hear it every day: "Investors scared off by unemployment numbers as the Dow drops 150 points" or "Dow up 250 points as

166

investors encouraged by European Central Bank debt reduction." Investors? You? Aunt Sandy? Brother Gabriel? Sister Caity? Well, unless you or your relatives and friends day trade, you all simply sit back and track your portfolio up and down while the stock market casino either has bells ringing for a slot machine win, or the dealer (a.k.a. investor) rakes in your chips. At a real casino, you at least exert some control—blackjack or poker skills, leaving a slot machine that you feel is a loser, or just plain walking out with some money in your pocket. Not so at the stock market casino. Unless you day trade or cash in your portfolio, usually at a loss, you have no control.

Here's how it works in the real-world stock market casino, possibly exaggerating the ends to make the point.

YEAR	DOW
1954	381
1987	2,700
1995	4,000
2001 (pre-9/11)	11,000+
2002	7,000+
2007	14,000+
2009	6,500
Late 2014	17,000+
2018	24,000

Not shown in the above chart, the Dow skirted between the low hundreds and two thousand from 1900 to 1954, where it hovered at 381. So for the first half of the twentieth century, when very few of the middle class were investing (they were too busy trying to pay the rent, and fighting in two world wars, with many waiting on food lines in the 1930s), it was generally the wealthy who played with each other in the market, growing their wealth and power from the war machinery, economic growth following the wars, and international expansion.

But then the 1980s came along with a bonanza that changed the entire financial landscape, possibly the biggest domestic economic revolution ever—your 401K retirement plans. With the United States government's IRS providing pre-tax contributions and non-taxable income until it's withdrawn, it was a deal that most workers could not pass up. And, to sweeten the pot even more, many corporate employers matched your contributions. So if you put in, say, 6 percent of your salary every payday, your corporate employer might match it to a maximum amount. In essence, what you do every payday is play the stock market; except for the fact that most of you aren't selling, you're buying. Every payday, you increase the value of the stocks (and the stocks within the mutual funds) that you own. All as a legitimate means of being able to retire in comfort.

And did it ever look that way in the 1990s. Between your 401K contributions, the dot com revolution, and the wealthy buying stock, the market moved as it had never done in its history; the Dow increased by over 300 percent, from 2,700 in 1987 to over eleven thousand in pre–9/11, 2001, not even fifteen years. Talk about the ultimate bubble. And you, and Uncle Cody, and brother Henry, and sister Savannah were thrilled with your portfolio. As you should have been. Between the increase in the stocks you owned and your salary contributions, you were on the way to an easy retirement. God bless America; the American Dream had come true.

September 11 temporarily changed all that. Although the Dow was trending downward after the dot com bust, it plunged in the months following 9/11, bottoming out in the seven thousands. You and your friends and family lost a lot of your retirement, probably roughly 30 percent! If your portfolio had been worth $150,000, it had dropped to around $100,000 within a year after the Twin Towers collapsed. What happened to that $50,000? Did it disappear? Did GE, or GM, or Yahoo go out of business? No, what happened to at least most of that $50,000 is it went into the coffers of the wealthy, and here's how.

The wealth of the richest people in the world is staggering, well into the trillions of dollars. And what do they do with that sum of money—buy five-year CDs at less than 1 percent interest? No. They invest it in companies all around the globe, in investment firms and hedge funds, and their money is invested and then sold at their whim. When they bought stock in 1987, 1990, or 1995, and sold it in 2001 to 2002, each one most likely made untold billions from those investments. Think about it. If just one of them bought $500,000 worth of Wells Fargo stock in 1987 and sold it in October 2001 when the market had gone up 300 percent, they conceivably could have made $1.5 million in profit from that one sale if Wells Fargo stock had trended exactly as the Dow did in those fourteen years. Remember, you most likely did not sell your Wells Fargo stock in October 2001. You were sitting tight like most, so your loss went right into the financial accounts of the wealthy.

The American worker was set up in the 1980s. Nixon's total and complete elimination of the gold standard made the introduction of a money supply into the economy that enabled the market to expand, and in conjunction with the billions in investments from the 401Ks, created a bubble the likes of which had never been seen until after the recovery from the financial implosion of 2008. Never before in the history of the United States was the financial livelihood of America's middle-class workers placed in a lottery where the wealthy controlled the winning numbers.

From 2002 to 2007, the market went up almost 100 percent. If the wealthy took one-half or all of that profit they made in 2001 to 2002, poured it back into the market in the five or so years from 2002 to 2007, and then sold those shares causing the market to plunge in 2009 following the 2008 financial disaster, how much money did they again make? And so on.

And, ultra-wealthy investors don't trade during the day. Oh no, they have made it so that all day-traders have twenty-four-hour access to the stock market. You've heard the term "futures." This is the trading that has occurred in the middle of the night while you're sleeping. You can conceivably wake up at eight in the morning to find you have made 3 percent in the market or lost 2 percent. At least in a real casino they don't take your money while you sleep.

The middle class, excluding the day traders, are in a casino where they can't possibly win. Gambling casinos are stacked toward the house, but, as has been pointed out, you do have some control. Unless you're a day trader, you're no more than a sitting duck, just waiting for wealthy investors (which include corporations, by the way) to cash in their stocks and take your money.

And if it hasn't happened by the time you're reading this, it will happen soon—another "correction" of the market where you'll lose another 20 or 30 percent or whatever. The 401Ks finally gave the wealthy ownership of your bank. You're simply a depositor of your life's savings, and they decide when to make withdrawals of your money. Don't forget that George W. Bush and the Republican platform in the 2000s was for Social Security to be privatized. Not only would they then have access to your 401K deposits, but they would completely control your retirement.

The New Silk Road Led Right to 9/11

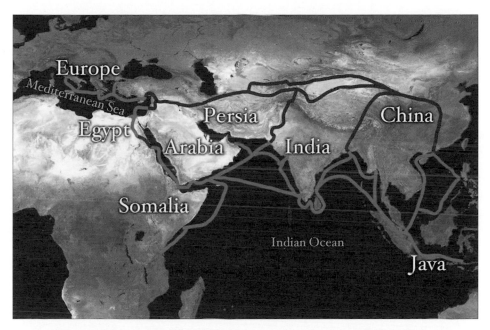

The land and sea routes of the four thousand-mile old silk road of centuries ago where East and West traded products and cultures. The new silk road had to do with an LNG (liquid natural gas) pipeline, leading to Enron's demise and 9/11. Splette, NASA Goddard Space Flight Center, 2010.

It has not been a secret that George W. Bush and Enron CEO Ken Lay had a close relationship for years. As a matter of fact, Lay and Enron contributed $550,000 to Bush's many campaigns.[146] It has been alleged that in 1988, soon after George H. W. Bush assumed the presidency, either George W. Bush or his brother Neil called Argentina's minister of public works in an attempt to pressure him into awarding a $300 million contract to Enron. Argentine politician Rudolfo Terragno recalled that he was told that the Enron project "would be very favorable for Argentina and its relations with the United States."[147]

Enron, along with Bechtel and General Electric, spent an enormous amount of money to build a power plant in Dabhol, India, even though the World Bank warned that the electricity produced would be too expensive to justify the costs. Unable to secure an oil deal with Qatar which would have furnished the necessary affordable energy, Enron now desperately depended on a pipeline from the oil-rich Caspian region, through Afghanistan, to India in order for the power plant to be successful.

In 1996, the US company Unocal began negotiating with the Taliban to build the pipeline. Following unsuccessful meetings held in Argentina and the United States, a consortium was formed with Unocal, Saudi Arabia's Delta Oil Company, and groups in Japan, Korea, Indonesia, Pakistan, and Turkmenistan called CentGas (Central Asian Gas Pipeline), and the talks continued for TAP, the Turkmenistan Afghanistan Pipeline.[148] The important thing to remember is that it mattered little to Enron which company built the pipeline, or the route that it took, just that it got built in order to ensure the success of the Dabhol power plant, and the profit potential from the venture.

The 1998 Kenya bombings, with known Taliban links to the bombers, for all intents and purposes put an end to discussions with the Taliban. President Clinton bombed Taliban sites in Afghanistan and placed pressure on Unocal to cease and desist pipeline communications.[149] Enron's power plant was in serious trouble. The Human Rights Watch organization reported that environmentalists and employee organizations demonstrating against the plant were subjected to inhuman retaliatory tactics by the plant officials such as beatings, detentions, and not being paid. Saying that it was too expensive,

India's State Board of Electricity stopped paying Enron for the power supply, and in June 2001, terminated its agreement with Enron.[150]

So less than three months before 9/11, Enron closed the plant, and the much-heralded secret and private White House meetings between Enron and Vice President Cheney were held in 2001. Here we are with newly-elected president George W. Bush, after receiving large campaign contributions from both Enron and Ken Lay, along with newly-elected vice president Dick Cheney, former head of Halliburton, actively campaigning for Enron.

Both the New York *Daily News* and the *Washington Post* revealed a "Dabhol Working Group," with the National Security Council in the Summer of 2001, just weeks prior to 9/11. Enron was apparently so important to the economic and political interests of the country because their investment would be lost, and bankruptcy was at-hand.[151]

John O'Neill was an FBI counter-terrorism expert in 2001, and privately discussed White House obstruction during his Osama Bin Laden investigation, noting that the US was still keeping the idea open of a possible Taliban pipeline deal.[152]

Michael C. Ruppert in his book *Crossing the Rubicon*, offers a very interesting timeline:

- August 2, 2001: State Department director of Asian affairs meets secretly with the Taliban ambassador in a last-minute attempt at negotiating a pipeline.
- September 11, 2001: The 9/11 attacks.
- October 9, 2001: Almost exactly a month later, US Ambassador Wendy Chamberlain meets with the Pakistani oil minister and is briefed on the gas pipeline project from Turkmenistan, through Afghanistan, and into Pakistan.
- December 22, 2001: Prime Minister Hamid Karzai, a previous Unocal paid consultant and a prior Taliban deputy foreign minister, takes over in Afghanistan.
- February 9, 2002: Karzai and the president of Pakistan announce that they have agreed to "cooperate in all spheres of activity," which includes the pipeline since it is considered to be "in the interest of both countries."

- February 14, 2002: Israeli newspaper columnist Uri Averny notes that the current map of Afghanistan shows that US airbases built since the attack are identical to the projected route of the oil pipeline.[153]

Those lucky sons of bitches—9/11 came along, and the United States and its Western Allies gained total control of Afghanistan—that precious piece of real estate that was needed to pump the West's natural gas from Turkmenistan and the Caspian Region, through Afghanistan, south into Pakistan and finally into India. It was too late for Enron, but just in the nick of time for the United States of America and its Western allies.

Was building the pipeline, and bailing out Enron, the reasons that United States troops didn't simply invade Afghanistan, kill or capture Bin Laden, and get the hell out so our soldiers could be home for Thanksgiving? Or was this just another instance of, as Smedley said, soldiers following the dollar?

From 500 BC to 1500 AD, there was a 4,000 mile stretch of roads that served as an interstate between the centers of civilization in Europe and the Middle East and onward into India and China, which shaped the culture and history of both the European and Asian peoples. This was the Silk Road, and upon completion, the modern Silk Road will become the source of oil between East and West, controlled by the United States. Called the Trans-Afghanistan Pipeline, or TAPI, the pipeline agreement was signed in 2013 to go from Turkmenistan, through Afghanistan, into Pakistan, ending in India. Construction began in December 2015, the Afghanistan section was started in 2018, and the entire pipeline will most likely be completed in 2019 or 2020, approximately two decades after the Twin Towers, the Pentagon, and four packed commercial jetliners lost around three thousand lives.

1999: The Repeal of the Glass-Steagall Act

Essentially enacted by FDR to prevent another financial catastrophe, the Glass-Steagall Act of 1933 prevented banks from investing in securities, completely separating them from investment banks. And it worked, until 1999, when Congressional legislators, in conjunction with a $300 million lobbying effort by the banks and every corporation who would make untold profit from eliminating Glass-Steagall, removed that barrier from the banking industry, setting the stage for the financial disaster of 2008, and the subsequent bailing out of the financial institutions that were victims of their own greed.

Although other factors were almost certainly involved, such as the wars in Afghanistan and Iraq, and the bursting of the dot-com bubble, the repeal of Glass-Steagall set the stage for the financial devastation of 2008. How did the Federal Reserve, that same economic brain trust that along with FDR and his legislators enacted Glass-Steagall to prevent another financial atrocity, allow the repeal of that same act seventy years later, watching as the bankers and financial institutions swallowed up all of those mortgage-backed securities? How did those economic and financial giants on the Federal Reserve Board not know that the same banking practices that caused the Great Depression would again cause economic and social devastation in 2008 and beyond, just as it did in 1929?

President Trump is reportedly looking into bringing back Glass-Steagall.

9/11

Most Americans at least have an inkling as to what the mood of the country had been on December 7, 1941, when the Japanese destroyed the Hawaiian fleet, killing 2,400 of our servicemen. But the 2,992 victims of 9/11 possibly evoke even more outrage. As devastating as it was, the Pearl Harbor attack was a military aggression and engagement. On 9/11, the dead were almost all civilians in their workplace at the World Trade Center, at the Pentagon, on airplanes slamming into buildings at hundreds of miles an hour, with one allegedly nose-diving into a field, and hundreds of New York City firefighters not only doing their job of putting out fires but also trying to save the lives of at least some of the civilian victims. FDR coined December 7, 1941, as the "Day of Infamy"; 9/11 is simply "9/11."

Forty-eight hours after the attacks began, the FBI announced the names of the eighteen, and soon changed to nineteen, Islamic Al-Qaeda terrorists who were split into four hijacking squads. President Bush immediately declared a War on Terrorism, and soon thereafter, Afghanistan and Iraq were attacked in the name of 9/11 and terrorism. September 11, and the ensuing Anthrax "terrorist" attack, shocked Americans into a state of mind whereby they could not fathom how this could happen on their soil; shocked into a state of mind where their leaders became heroes, and the military became personal weapons of revenge. Americans willingly gave them carte blanche.

The events of 9/11 won't be rehashed here. The author's thesis is the almost likely aspect that the events of 9/11 were either made to happen or allowed to happen, duplicating similar maneuvers in the last century to invoke hate and fear in order to rally the American

Firefighter in front of burning building and rubble following September 11, 2001, terrorist attack on World Trade Center, New York City. Mike Goad.

people against an enemy for the purpose of waging war for profits and military strategic placement.

Architect Richard Gage, AIA, is the founder and president of Architects & Engineers for 9/11 Truth (AE911Truth). Beginning in 2006, this nonprofit organization of architects, engineers, and affiliates has dedicated itself to establishing the truth about the events of September 11, 2001.

Mr. Gage has been an architect for thirty years, having worked on construction administration for a $125 million high school, and more recently, near Las Vegas, six blocks of retail and midrise office space, altogether about 1,200 tons of fireproofed steel framing. AE911Truth represents more than 3,000 architects and engineers demanding a new investigation into the destruction of the three World Trade Center towers.

The organization's purpose written on their website is to "Pursue our mission by conducting research and educating the public about the scientific evidence related to the destruction of the *three* World Trade Center towers, and by working with victims' families and other activists to advocate for a new investigation. At the heart of our work is our deeply-held conviction that establishing the truth is essential to achieving justice for the murder of nearly 3,000 people that day. Furthermore, we believe that an honest public accounting of 9/11 is the *only* way to bring about genuine and lasting change to the system that enabled this atrocity to take place and to the sweeping policies enacted in its aftermath."

The following are excerpts of a talk that Mr. Gage made in Switzerland in November 2018:[154]

. . . But you know, we're not here really just to talk about how three skyscrapers were destroyed. There is something much more important about this subject. . . . And that is that we've invaded two countries and killed a couple of million people in Afghanistan and Iraq. We have a $4.5 trillion ongoing global war on terror as a result of 9/11, and initiated by the events that occurred at the World Trade Center. We've lost civil liberties in our country. We can be arrested without just cause, and we can be held indefinitely without a right to a trial, a lawyer, or a jury.

The first thing we should note concerning the World Trade Center is Tower 7, comprised of forty-seven stories, the tallest buildings in most of the states of the US. It was part of the World Trade Center complex, about a football field away from the North Tower. When the Twin Towers came down, it got hit by some of the columns and beams that were ejected out of the towers, causing some fires, but it was standing just fine until about five-twenty in the afternoon. That's when the building collapsed—in just under seven seconds. A third of its fall was in free-fall acceleration.

The National Institute of Standards and Technology (NIST), assigned by Congress to investigate the collapses of the three towers, said that the Building 7 collapse was primarily due to uncontrolled fires. They focused their theory on one column underneath the east penthouse, because that penthouse came down six seconds prior to the overall building. Their theory of collapse was that this column gave way underneath the penthouse, and the rest of the building came down due to the failure of that one column.

AE911Truth has found that there have been dozens of much hotter, larger, and longer-lasting fires in high rises—such as a building in Los Angeles that burned for three and a half hours over five floors, and in Philadelphia, burning eighteen hours over eight floors, and in Venezuela, burning seventeen hours over twenty-six floors. Not one high-rise prior to 9/11 has collapsed due to fire. Yet on 9/11, we have three.

Let's look at what *can* bring buildings down, and what *has* brought buildings down intentionally and historically—controlled demolitions, because there are dozens of them every year. They place shaped cutter charges at the columns and beams around the building, and then detonate them in a very precise order—synchronistically-timed, floor-by-floor so that the building can come down symmetrically, if that's what they desire, or in any other way that they desire, and generally at or near freefall acceleration. This is not something that fire can do; it's something that only a handful of the top demolition companies in the world can handle.

There's a set of features associated with these controlled demolitions, which you'll see satisfy the features of destruction found in the three World Trade Center towers. Let's concentrate on the forty-seven floor Tower 7:

- SUDDEN ONSET of destruction—Building 7 began its collapse without any visible hesitation, which would be expected by a building impacting upon itself.
- STRAIGHT DOWN symmetrical collapse into building footprint—After the penthouse collapsed, the remaining building came down straight and symmetrical in under

seven seconds. For this to have happened, the core columns underneath that main penthouse had to have been taken out all at once—the twenty-four core columns, followed by the perimeters.

- PATTERNED REMOVAL OF COLUMN SUP-PORTS— How do they bring a building straight down? In the case of Tower 7, they have to remove those twenty-four core columns followed by those perimeter columns within a fraction of a second of each other— synchronistically timed floor-by-floor. Does fire have that level of precision, especially the few small scattered fires in Building 7?

- FREE-FALL ACCELERATION through the path of greatest resistance—How fast is Tower 7 coming down? Physics experts show us that it came down at free fall acceleration. But there's forty thousand tons of resistance holding this building up, which is three to five times stronger than is needed to hold it up for the life of the building. How did Building 7 fall at free-fall acceleration when it had forty thousand tons of resistance holding it up? In addition, falling at free fall means that not one of the Building 7 columns gave any resistance at all. Fire has never brought down a skyscraper, and fire could never have dislodged each of those twenty-four core columns at once.

- TOTAL SHATTERING of the structural steel frame—Tower 7 was a forty-seven-story steel frame building where most of the columns and the beams were rigidly welded to each other; yet they gave way like a house of cards, and it fell into a six-story pile. Buildings that fall naturally fall over, following the path of least resistance. They don't fall straight down through themselves. The beams and columns are not dismembered one from the other. The concrete is not pulverized to a fine powder.

- SOUNDS OF EXPLOSIONS heard by credible witnesses— Many witnesses reported hearing sounds of explosions and seeing flashes of light, yet NIST's final report did not include any of these hundreds of testimonies.

Fire, the government's official cause of destruction for the World Trade Center's demise, doesn't account for any one of these characteristics. Fires have caused less robust structures to collapse, and when they do so it's:

- Asymmetrical
- It is gradual. It follows the laws of entropy. It's chaotic.
- It would fall over, in stages.

To the more than 3,000 architects and engineers who belong to AE911Truth, this is proof that Tower 7 was brought down by controlled demolition.

The Twin Towers

The official story is that the combination of the plane collisions and the fires burning so hot caused the steel frame of each building to give way. Suddenly, and with no warning, 110 stories crumbled to the ground at almost free-fall acceleration in about twelve seconds.

The official story of the tower's collapse goes against every known theory of physics. The government says that the collapse of the top fifteen stories drove the rest of the tower down to the ground. When you watch a slow-motion video of the collapse, you will see that the top portion of each tower actually destroys itself in the first few seconds. After that, the top fifteen stories are gone. There's nothing left to crush the rest of the building down to the ground. What we might have seen if the official story was valid is the upper and lower sections mutually destroy each other until all the energy is dissipated and the system comes to rest. Alternatively, the top section could have fallen off to the side after the initial collapse, leaving the rest of the floors below intact. What could *not* have happened is that the lightest section of the building above could not have fallen and crushed all the floors below it. It is such a simple fundamental concept that architects and engineers were astonished in seeing it totally ignored by NIST.

Let's again apply the model of controlled demolition features and see if it applies or not to the Twin Towers collapse, just as we did Tower 7.

1. SUDDEN ONSET of destruction—Both towers were standing still, and then suddenly dropped smoothly. There's no jolt, hesitation, impact, or the entropy of falling over.

2. PATTERNED EXPLOSIONS and FLASHES OF LIGHT— We didn't know until August of 2005 that New York City had this treasure trove of testimonies orally recorded by the first responders in October of 2001. One hundred eighteen of the first responders observed flashes, sounds of explosions, and other phenomena indicative of explosive demolition. "All of a sudden the ground just started shaking. It felt like a train running under my feet. The next thing we know, we look up and the tower is collapsing." "Shortly before the first tower came down, I remember feeling the ground shaking. I heard a terrible noise and then debris just started flying everywhere." Assistant Fire Commissioner James Drury said, "I thought the terrorists planted explosives somewhere in the building. That's how loud it was . . . crackling explosive." Eyewitness after eyewitness describes "*boom, boom, boom*" or "*pop, pop, pop,*" exactly what it sounds like just prior to a building's collapse during controlled demolition. The official story is that the towers began their collapse *causing* all of that phenomena, yet the reality proven from the eyewitness accounts is that the collapse was the *result* of the explosive phenomena.

3. STRAIGHT-DOWN symmetrical progression *outside* footprint—There is a symmetrical progression that is straight down, but unlike Building 7, not *inside* the footprint—that was a perfect implosion—but this was a very *explosive*, symmetrical straight down event, but out 1,200 feet in diameter. We have symmetrical progression all the way down despite the asymmetry from the plane damage and the fires in the building. The steel structure is completely broken up well beyond

the boundary of The World Trade Center. By the way, if a hundred thousand tons of structural steel is delivered *outside* the footprint of each of the towers, then what's left to crush the building? The concrete floors? Stand by.

4. EJECTIONS OF BUILDING MATERIALS AT LOWER FLOORS —In the case of the South Tower, all at once, there are dozens of isolated explosive ejections known as squibs in the controlled demolition industry, indicating the complete disintegration of this top section, which is why it comes down in and on itself, and couldn't possibly drive the rest of the building down, because it's being destroyed from within. In addition, twenty, forty, and even sixty stories down, we see these "squibs" which are pulverized building materials. NIST says these are puffs of air being produced by that giant block of building pushing air down the elevator hoists that has got to go out somewhere. If this was the case, though, we would not have seen these highly focalized pinpoint accurate violent ejections occurring at 160 to 200 feet per second. These are explosive speeds.

5. FREE-FALL ACCELERATION through path of *greatest* resistance—There was most certainly near free fall acceleration of collapse in about twelve seconds, at about ten floors per second. Exact free-fall time would have been 9.2 seconds. There's not even time for those 280 columns to buckle on each floor.

6. TOTAL SHATTERING of the structural steel frame—The structural steel frame is almost completely shattered—all the way down to ground level.

7. LATERAL EJECTION of structural steel up to 600 feet at 60 mph—Flying structural steel sections landed up to 600 feet in every direction, blown out horizontally. If the building came down as the official story says, those steel sections would be brought *down* by gravity; not shot out *horizontally*, and with enough energy to fire a 200-pound ball, three miles. Where did all that energy come from?

8. Pyroclastic-like clouds of PULVERIZED CONCRETE— 110 stories fell in each tower. If you believe the official story, shouldn't Ground Zero have been comprised of 110 floors of debris stacked up in a pancake-like collapse? Yet all we have is a two, three, or four-story pile of core columns, perimeter columns, and other miscellaneous metal. Where are all the concrete floors? Each of them was an acre in size and there's 110 of them. We don't find fifty, we don't find ten, and we don't even find one. What happened to them? They're pulverized in midair *during the collapse.* All the photos and videos show us exactly what happened to 90,000 tons of concrete in each of these towers spread over lower Manhattan in a three-square-mile area. By the way, if ninety thousand tons of concrete is pulverized in midair and spread *outside* the perimeter of each building, what was left to crush the building? Certainly not the steel that was also *outside* the perimeter. So now it is *two-thirds of the weight of this building that is not even present to crush the building below, which is what the official story tells us!*

9. Persistent Extreme Heat MOLTEN STEEL/IRON—The National Fire Protection Association—Guide 921 says to look for extreme thermal effects in fire, because if you have that, then you have good reason to suspect incendiaries. "Large volumes of gas in the large amount of heat released in chemical explosions causing rapidly expanding plumes in cauliflower shapes." Exactly what was seen at the Twin Towers as they were destroyed. This was a lot more heat than was available at the time of the collapses, which was minimal, indicated by the thick black smoke clouds. These fires are oxygen-starved and diminished at the time of the collapse. So where is the extreme heat coming from? *Possibly the most important unexplained phenomenon at ground zero is the extremely high temperatures registered under the rock for many weeks after the collapses. Mayor Giuliani reported that underground fires were at temperatures of 2000 degrees Fahrenheit. The Journal of the American Society of*

Safety Engineers wrote that thermal measurements taken by helicopter each day, showed underground temperatures of more than 2,800 degrees Fahrenheit eight weeks later, and the fires still had not subsided. As a matter of fact, the last fire finally extinguished itself on December 19, 2001, more than 3.5 months after the collapse. Numerous eyewitnesses saw molten steel and iron, even calling it molten lava. Officials tried to say that it was aluminum or lead, but there are tons and tons of it, and aluminum and lead don't glow white-hot, which can be seen pouring out of the towers just prior to its collapse. FEMA reported that "a liquid eutectic mixture containing primarily *iron*, oxygen, and sulfur formed during this hot corrosion attack on the steel. . . . No clear explanation for the source of the sulfur has been identified." [See #10 below.] In fact, the *New York Times* called it "the deepest mystery uncovered in the investigation," but was completely eliminated from the NIST report. How do we get those kinds of temperatures? The fires are only said to be about 1,200 degrees Fahrenheit. Hydrocarbons—which is what building materials and jet fuel are—only burn 600 to 1,400 degrees Fahrenheit. How then did all of that steel melt when it takes 2,800 degrees Fahrenheit to melt steel? What could cause those high temperatures?

10. Forensic evidence of THERMITE INCENDIARIES— Thermite is a very effective means of destroying steel structures, more effective than explosives. In just two seconds, thermite reaches temperatures of 4,500 degrees Fahrenheit. And sulfur, combined with thermite, produces thermate, which is much more effective at cutting through steel. If thermite were used, it would explain the presence of molten iron. And, if thermite were used, it would have produced a characteristic burn pattern; a white, yellow hot liquid which can be seen pouring out of the South Tower. It would also produce a whitish cloud of aluminum oxide ash which can be seen rising off the top of that molten metal. And, regarding those freely flying structural steel members, why are their ends trailed by thick white

smoke clouds? Structural steel is not combustible in office fires with jet fuel. The US Geological Survey performed studies on the World Trade Center dust, and found amounts to billions of previously molten iron microspheres—about the diameter of a human hair. They can't explain where they came from, yet these molten iron microspheres just happen to be byproducts of thermite reactions, and they were formed *during* the event; not before and not after, but *during*.

Almost as soon as the book *9/11 Revealed: The Unanswered Questions* by Ian Henshall and Morgan Rowland was released, the United States Department of State Information website, International Information programs, contained a section titled, "9/11 Revealed, New Book Repeats False Conspiracy Theories." This article was on their website for years but has since been removed. It included the following statements:

> *9/11 Revealed*, published in August 2005, is the latest book putting forth bizarre conspiracy theories about the September 11, 2001, terrorist attacks on the United States. Its two British authors, Ian Henshall and Rowland Morgan, give credence to a hodgepodge of sinister, unfounded allegations. . . .
>
> The book claims the World Trade Center (WTC) Twin Towers collapsed because they were pre-rigged with explosives but ignores an extraordinarily thorough, three-year investigation by the US National Institute for Standards and Technology (NIST).[155] NIST concluded the towers collapsed because the impact of the plane crashes severed and damaged support columns and dislodged fireproofing insulation from the steel floor trusses and support columns, which allowed the fires to weaken them to the point where they bowed, buckled, and failed. It stated on its website that it found "no corroborating evidence for alternative hypotheses suggesting that the WTC towers were brought down by controlled demolition. . . . The book suggests that the 47-story World Trade Center 7 building, which also collapsed on September 11, was intentionally demolished. . . ."

The first thing that must be noted is that the Warren Commission that investigated the JFK assassination and the nine Congressional commissions that investigated Pearl Harbor during and after World War II were both obviously inaccurate in their conclusions. A multitude of evidence has been brought out to-date disproving the conclusions of these former commissions, so there is no reason to believe that the NIST conclusions are any more reliable than those of its predecessors.

Furthermore, if Tower 7 was not brought down, it was the only steel-structured skyscraper in the history of the world to be destroyed by fire, falling just one-half second longer than if it was a freefalling penny with no air resistance.[156]

- If the World Trade Center collapsed due to structural damage caused by the planes, why didn't the portion of the Pentagon hit by the Boeing 757 collapse for the same reason?
- Did the NIST staff verify that they were examining pieces of the steel girders from the WTC towers?
- If the steel girders examined by the NIST staff were from the towers, wouldn't a controlled demolition also have dislodged fireproofing insulation coating the steel floor trusses and steel columns?
- What happened to all of the ninety floors of desks, file cabinets, sheetrock, elevators, and most importantly, *the black boxes from the two hijacked planes*?
- Why were the remaining portions of the steel girders hauled away immediately and shipped to the Far East to be melted down? Those steel girders were evidence.
- The State Department's information site stated, "The book claims a drone Boeing 757, or a smaller plane painted in American Airlines colors, hit the Pentagon, but ignores the fact that forensic specialists identified the crew and passengers of American Airlines flight 77 from remains found in the Pentagon, proving irrefutably that the flight hit the Pentagon." How did the forensic specialists know that the remains came from the Pentagon and not from somewhere else?
- There were three known videos taken of the "hit" at the

Pentagon. One was from a hotel roof, another from a gas station directly across from the Pentagon, and the last from a civilian. All three were immediately confiscated by FBI agents and never returned.

• Why did the Al-Qaeda terrorist pilot make an unusually difficult 330-degree turn and then approach the Pentagon from almost ground level—both maneuvers very difficult even for an experienced pilot—and attack the exact portion of the Pentagon that had been under construction with a limited amount of personnel? For maximum damage and minimum ease, why didn't he approach the Pentagon as a Japanese kamikaze pilot would have, smack dab in the middle, taking out the maximum number of army personnel and virtually destroying

This is a composite of several images of the president and his national security team during a series of meetings in the Situation Room of the White House discussing the mission against Osama bin Laden on Sunday, May 1, 2011. We put this together so in addition to the previous, now-iconic image of this day, people might have a better sense of what it's like in presidential meetings of historic significance. Official White House Photo by Pete Souza.

the heart of the war mechanism? And, using the NIST results, the structural damage would almost certainly have brought down the Pentagon.

Finally, the State Department's information site stated: "The book takes the bizarre position that the September 11 attacks were not real terrorist attacks and were somehow designed to 'limit casualties.' Apparently, the largest terrorist event in history was not large enough to convince the book's authors that it was real."[157]

Osama Bin Laden and his Al-Qaeda terrorists planned an ingenious and near-flawless attack, taking out nearly 3000 of our citizens and causing billions of dollars in property damage. The only flaw turned out to be Flight 93, which was presumably headed for the White House but wound up crashing in a Pennsylvania field. Yes, it was the largest terrorist attack in American history, but from Bin Laden's perspective, the results should have been far worse. An Al-Qaeda video shows Bin Laden laughing that the towers went down, which he almost certainly did not expect, but killing three thousand people was minuscule compared to what was possible.

The two planes that slammed into the World Trade Center took off at around eight in the morning with a minimum number of passengers, but more importantly, the impacts occurred at 8:48 a.m. and 9:03 a.m. If the perpetrators had hijacked planes at nine in the morning, hitting the towers an hour later, they would have been filled with thousands more employees, and many more would have been killed. Why didn't the terrorists schedule their attack later in the day when they could have killed thousands more?

Again, why did the inexperienced Al-Qaeda pilot bother with very difficult maneuvers when he could have simply dive-bombed the Pentagon, taking all or most of it out, killing many more people, and more importantly, possibly taking out the heart of the nation's military apparatus?

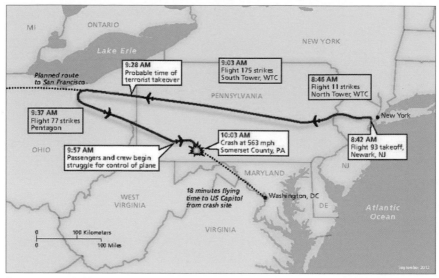

Route map of Flight 93, which includes a timeline of events starting with the takeoff in Newark. US National Park Service, restoration/cleanup by Matt Holly, 2017.

SOME FURTHER QUESTIONS:

- The anthrax used in the attack immediately following 9/11 was ultimately found to have come from a US facility located in Maryland. Was this attack to further terrorize and panic America's citizens and divert attention away from investigation into the events surrounding 9/11?

- Was Operation Northwoods, the proposal by the Joint Chiefs to down a drone plane over Cuba, the inspiration for 9/11? The Joint Chiefs were prepared to do it in 1962. What would prevent them from carrying it out forty years later?

- NORAD had been engaged in week-long war games called Operation Vigilant Guardian when 9/11 occurred. Were the Arab terrorists so aware of America's activities that they scheduled an attack when their actions might possibly be confused by NORAD as a game, slowing down US reaction time?

- A large piece of one of the engines of Flight 93, which crashed into a Pennsylvania field, was found a mile away from the crash site, possibly indicating that the plane did not crash, but had instead been shot down. If the plane had been shot down,

September 11 attacks. The Twin Towers from Greenwich Street after United Airlines Flight 175 crashed into WTC2. Hans Joachim Dudeck, 2009.

Image of plane (highlighted) hitting the Pentagon. Washington, DC (Pentagon 9/11 security video). US Government Security Camera, September 11, 2001.

why was it kept a secret? Could it have been to add a "luster" of Americans fighting for their lives? Was it a coincidence that the rallying cry of the Afghanistan attack was "Let's roll!" the famous last words of the cell phone conversation from on-board Flight 93?

- Mohammad Atta boarded a plane in Portland, Maine, bound for Boston, and then got on a connecting flight to New York City. Atta had been carousing in Boston the night before. Why did he drive the hour and a half up to Portland just to take a flight to Boston? Was it because he knew that Boston's Logan Airport had no surveillance cameras and he wanted to be photographed by the Portland Airport cameras? Was this worth it? If the Portland to Boston flight had been delayed, the entire operation would have had to be scrapped and rescheduled? At Logan Airport, Atta's suitcase was left off his flight. In the suitcase were Islamic maps, flying instruction booklets, and other items to help identify the terrorists. Even with all of the lost luggage during flights, isn't it a million to one shot that Atta's suitcase would have been the one left off his flight? It's obvious that it was left off for identification purposes, but if Atta did this intentionally, did he have an accomplice working in baggage at Logan, or did operatives take care of it for him?

- Though there appears to be conflicting evidence, in 2001 it was nearly impossible for a cell phone connection to go higher than an altitude of 10,000 feet, which means that each cell phone conversation almost certainly could not possibly have occurred when the planes were flying at cruising altitudes over 30,000 feet.

- A few hours after the Twin Towers had collapsed, on or around 1:00 p.m. EDT, ABC News Anchor Peter Jennings conducted a phone interview with New York City Mayor Rudy Giuliani from the Mayor's temporary office in midtown New York. Remarkably, at exactly 1:50 p.m. of the interview, Mayor Giuliani told Mr. Jenkins, "When we were told that the World Trade Center was going to collapse . . ." An extraordinary comment considering three things: With hundreds of firefighters and police not only in the immediate vicinity of the Twin Towers, but inside on the stairwells conducting their rescue operations, why weren't these firemen and the police not notified of the impending collapse so they could evacuate? Who told the Mayor that the towers would collapse, especially in light of the fact that not one skyscraper had ever collapsed from fire? And lastly, why would Mr. Giuliani ever have made this statement to a major network if it wasn't true? The mayor has countless times since denied ever saying this, even in the face of this video being available for viewing, and the 9/11 commission never questioned Mr. Giuliani about this admission, and so it was not placed into the public record.

- Possibly the most important question—if it's true that the government fabricated the official story, why did they need to bring down a forty-seven-story building that really had nothing to do with 9/11? The hijacking of the commercial airliners, the government's military installation at the Pentagon hit by one of the planes, and two of the hijacked planes slamming into the Twin Towers with the ensuing collapse, killing almost 3,000 people, were all that was needed to justify the invasions of Afghanistan and Iraq, the ensuing regime-removals, the installation of strategic United States military bases, the oil companies resuming their role in Iraq's oil production, TAPI, and the ensuing massive profits. With no added loss of life to the final body count, why did Tower 7 have to be destroyed, especially since many Americans aren't even aware that it not only existed but that it collapsed along with the Twin Towers? Could it have been the central network hub for planning this 9/11 false flag operation?

Let's ask some questions, and find some possible answers and motives to this last point:

- Who occupied thirty-seven of those forty-seven floors in Tower 7? Answer: Salomon Smith Barney
- Who was chairman of the Salomon Smith Barney International Advisory Board prior to becoming George W. Bush's secretary of state? Answer: Donald Rumsfeld[158]

- Who was on the International Advisory Board of Salomon Smith Barney prior to becoming George W. Bush's vice president? Answer: Dick Cheney[159]
- Who also occupied floors in Tower 7? Answer: A Secret CIA office,[160] NYC Office of Emergency Management, The Department of Defense, and the US Secret Service.[161]

Need we say more?

Recent Secret History

With his family by his side, Barack Obama is sworn in as the 44th president of the United States by Chief Justice John G. Roberts, Jr. in Washington, DC, January 20, 2009. Master Sgt. Cecilio Ricardo, US Air Force.

President Obama was inaugurated on January 20, 2009, arguably the first president in the history of the country since George Washington to enter office with a clear mandate, even without winning a landslide vote.

January 21, 2009, one day after taking office, millions are out of work, losing their homes, a huge portion of their retirement savings, and have very little hope. Not too many US citizens had been around to remember the Great Depression, but many were now able to identify. These were Obama's appointees to the financial sector of his administration almost as soon as he was sworn in:

- Secretary of the Treasury: Timothy Geithner, former president of the New York Fed, one of the top financial people in the world responsible for red-flagging Wall Street. If he couldn't see that financial crisis coming, how would he see a future crisis coming? And among Geithner's decisions as head of the NY Fed—he helped design the $30 billion bailout of Bear Stearns for their mortgage securities fiasco.
- Geithner's Chief of Staff: Mark Patterson, former Goldman lobbyist.
- One of the administration's top economic advisers until 2010 was Lewis Sachs, former Chairman of the Mariner Investment Group (Tricadia), a company that allegedly sold CDOs (collateralized debt obligations) and then bet against these mortgage-based securities.
- The Commodity Futures Trading Commission is an independent agency that regulates the futures and options markets. Who did Obama pick as its head? Gary Gensler, also a former employee of Goldman. More importantly, though, the president chose one of those responsible for allowing

President Barack Obama talks with Treasury Secretary Timothy F. Geithner at the conclusion of a meeting in the Cabinet Room of the White House. Nov. 4, 2010. Official White House Photo by Pete Souza.

financial institutions to deal in derivatives (mortgage securities) by promoting the passage of the Commodities Futures Modernization Act of 2000, following the repeal of Glass-Steagall in 1999, exempting these over-the-counter derivatives from government regulation.

- Securities and Exchange Commission: FDR established this federal agency to regulate the stock market and the companies that trade on them. In other words, the SEC looks after the entire securities industry. Who did Obama select to head the commission? Mary Shapiro, the head of FINRA (Financial Industry Regulatory Agency). From the FINRA website: "FINRA's mission is to safeguard the investing public against fraud and bad practices. We pursue that mission by writing and enforcing rules and regulations for every single brokerage firm and broker in the United States, and by examining broker-dealers for compliance with our own rules, federal securities laws and rules of the Municipal Securities Rulemaking Board." Obama picked the head of the agency that was unsuccessful in protecting investors prior to the financial crisis to be the head of the commission that would regulate the stock market for possibly the next eight years.
- Former Clinton administration Treasury Secretary Larry Summers: his notoriety with the 2008 financial collapse was that, at the turn of this century, he was responsible, along with Chairman of the Federal Reserve Alan Greenspan, for spearheading the passage of the Commodities Futures Modernization Act, which as you already know made it legal for companies to deal in derivatives, causing the housing bubble and subsequent massive foreclosures. Why did the president of the United States choose one of the men responsible for the 2008 financial debacle as his chief economic advisor? Why didn't Obama choose someone like Brooksley Born, former head of the CFTC who wanted derivatives to be regulated and who was ousted by pressure precipitated by both Greenspan and Summers? Or Harvard Law School Professor Elizabeth Warren, whose life work has been bankruptcy law

and fighting for the middle class and consumer rights. Now a senator from the state of Massachusetts, *Time* magazine has called her "a new sheriff of Wall Street."

Not surprisingly, neither Congress nor the Department of Justice made any arrests, and no firms were prosecuted for financial fraud concerning the 2008 financial disaster. Millions of Americans lost their homes, their retirement money, their pride. Not one responsible person paid the price for this travesty and tragedy. That is Obama's legacy.

★

Although 94 percent of Americans polled in a June 2017 Quinnipiac University poll answered "yes" to the question, "Do you support or oppose requiring background checks for all gun buyers,"[162] the NRA has arguably never been more powerful. Immediately after the Parkland, Florida school shooting in February 2018, NRA head Wayne LaPierre said, "If these so-called European socialists take over the House and the Senate and, God forbid, they win the White House again our American freedoms could be lost and our country will be changed forever, and the first to go will be the Second Amendment to the US Constitution."

The Second Amendment: "A well-regulated Militia, being necessary to the security of a free State, the right of the people to keep and bear Arms, shall not be infringed."

What if the founding fathers were way ahead of their time and formulated a Second Amendment like this: "A well-regulated highway system, being necessary to the welfare of America's transportation structure and economy, the right of the people to keep and drive automobiles."

Is it feasible that if LaPierre was the head of the fictional National Automobile and Drivers Association that the NADA would be against states registering each and every automobile and issuing license plates for those vehicles, for every driver to take both a written and a driving test to make certain that they can drive properly and know the law of the road, that owners must have their vehicles regularly inspected so our roads are as safe as can be, that speed limits should be set so that drivers don't drive at excessive speeds on inferior roads or in densely populated areas, that seat belts should be worn for driver and passenger safety, and that drivers must have their headlights on at night so they can see properly. And potentially worst of all—will the Second Amendment be in jeopardy if drivers aren't allowed to drive under the influence?

In 2018, according to many polls, two out of three American citizens, for the most part, favor the Second Amendment, yet want the necessary controls to the ownership of guns so that our workplaces and schools are safer.

Current Secret History

With his family by his side, Donald Trump is sworn in as the 45th president of the United States by Chief Justice of the United States John G. Roberts Jr. in Washington, DC, Jan. 20, 2017.

Even many Trump supporters fully understand that his claims of "Fake News" is simply a method by him and his administration to rally his base into not questioning some of the absurdities that Trump has claimed both pre and post his first term in office.

Without a doubt, Trump himself has uttered quite a few fake news items.

But as you now hopefully can see after reading *America's Secret History*, the truth is that America's media has most certainly been the mecca of fake news.

Where was America's free press media during the King family 1999 civil lawsuit against the government? Where were the headlines on the front pages of every American newspaper the very next day shouting that a jury of twelve African American and white jurors found the government guilty of killing MLK?

Where were the headlines after Sirhan B. Sirhan was denied parole for the sixteenth time for the murder of RFK, when credible evidence presented at the parole hearing showed that he was not the killer?

Where were the editorials in all the major US newspapers and radio and television outlets calling for the posthumous impeachment of President Lyndon Baines Johnson when Ellsberg's Pentagon papers were released showing that the President lied to Congress and the American people concerning the Gulf of Tonkin incident, illegally and immorally escalating a war that killed millions of people?

Where were the editorials in all the major US newspapers and radio and television outlets calling for the impeachment of George W. Bush after he illegally took the country into war with Iraq when every UN observer found no WMD's or any evidence of terrorist activities?

Where were the newspaper and magazine articles and TV and radio commentators questioning the loopholes in the official story of the 2013 Boston Massacre arrest of the two Muslim brothers?

And, of course, the height of fake news— the Yellow Journalism of the late 1890s where two New York newspaper owners exaggerated, and in some cases, fabricated news, which incited America's citizens to endorse the imperialistic war of 1898.

Until America's media owns up to its responsibility to report the truths behind the stories, America's secret history will continue.

ENDNOTES

11   Howard K. Beale, *Theodore Roosevelt and the Rise of America to World Power* (Baltimore: John Hopkins University Press, 1956), 7.

12   Caproasia, "Global Rich List 2017—Huron Report," *Caproasia,* March 17, 2017, http://www.caproasia.com/2017/03/17/global-rich-list-2017-hurun-report/.

13   "Forbes: Nets and Barclays Center worth $1.8 Billion," *SB Nation,* February 15, 2017, https://www.netsdaily.com/2017/2/15/14628396/forbes-nets-and-presumably-barclays-center-worth-1-8-billion.

14   Rene A. Wormser, *Foundations: Their Power and Influence* (New York: Devin-Adair, 1958), vii-viii.

15   Wormser, back cover.

16   "The Report of Norman Dodd, Director of Research covering his direction of the staff of The Special Committee of The House of Representatives to Investigate Tax Exempt Foundations for the six months' period November 1, 1953—April 30, 1954," H. Rept. 2681, 83d Cong., 2d sess., Serial 11748, May 10, 1954.

17   William H. McIlhany II, *The Tax-Exempt Foundations,* from McIlhany's Dodd interview transcript (Arlington House, 1980), 60.

18   McIlhany, 60–61.

19   Ibid, 61.

20   Ibid, 62.

21   The Dodd Report to the Reece Committee on Foundations, April 29, 1954.

22   The Dodd Report to the Reece Committee on Foundations, April 29, 1954.

23   McIlhany, 73.

24   Ibid, 243–44.

25   House of Representatives, Special Committee to Investigate the Tax-Exempt Foundations, 1954.

26   Thomas M. McNiece, Testimony before the Reese Committee on Tax-Exempt Foundations, June 3, 1954.

27   Mark Preston, "CNN/ORC Poll: most think Congress is worst in their lifetime," CNN Politics, September 10, 2014, http://www.cnn.com/2014/09/09/politics/cnn-poll-congress/index.html.

28   "Beyond Distrust: How Americans View Their Government," Pew Research Center: US Politics & Policy, November 23, 2015, http://www.people-press.org/2015/11/23/beyond-distrust-how-americans-view-their-government/.

29   Cristiano Lima, "Gallup poll: Majority of Americans now favor more gun laws," *Politico,* November 9, 2015, https://www.politico.com/story/2017/11/09/gun-control-gallup-poll-244759.

30   Al Weaver and Susan Ferrechio, "Republicans reject Democratic calls for immediate vote on gun control," *Washington Examiner* Magazine Digital Edition, October 3, 2017, http://www.washingtonexaminer.com/re-publicans-reject-democratic-calls-for-immediate-vote-on-gun-control/article/2636342.

31   Heard on *All Things Considered,* "How Congress Quietly Overhauled Its Insider-Trading Law," Politics News from NPR, April 16, 2013, https://www.npr.org/sections/itsallpolitics/2013/04/16/177496734/how-congress-quietly-overhauled-its-insider-trading-law.

32   Ibid.

33   Nathaniel Blumberg, "The Afternoon of March 30," http://archive.is/2OHEI.

34   Blumberg.

35   Ibid.

36   Ibid.

37   Ibid.

38   Michele McPhee, "Whoever Built the Boston Marathon Bombs is Still on the Loose, Able to Kill Again," *Newsweek* Online, January 11, 2018, http://www.newsweek.com/2018/01/19/boston-marathon-bomb-maker-loose-776742.html.

39   "Tax havens: The missing $20 trillion, How to stop companies and people dodging tax, in Delaware as well as Grand Cayman," *The Economist,* February 16, 2013, https://www.economist.com/news/leaders/21571873-how-stop-companies-and-people-dodging-tax-delaware-well-grand-cayman-missing-20.

40 "Fortune 500 Companies Hold a Record $2.6 Trillion Offshore," Institute on Taxation and Economic Policy (ITEP), March 28, 2017, https://itep.org/fortune-500-companies-hold-a-record-26-trillion -offshore/.

41 Jeremy Bogaisky, "Burger King Gets Assist From Warren Buffett To Buy Tim Hortons," Forbes, August 25, 2014, https://www.forbes .com/sites/jeremybogaisky/2014/08/25/burger-king-may-get-an-as -sist-from-warren-buffett-in-purchase-of-tim-hortons/#5d076f1574e6.

42 Matthew Klein, "How many US manufacturing jobs were lost to glo-balization?," Financial Times, December 6, 2016, https://ftalphaville .ft.com/2016/12/06/2180771/how-many-us-manufacturing-jobs -were-lost-to-globalisation/.

43 Jeremy C. Owens, "Apple really isn't sitting on $216 billion in cash," MarketWatch, January 27, 2016, https://www.marketwatch.com /story/apple-isnt-really-sitting-on-216-billion-in-cash-2016-01-26.

44 Aimee Picchi, "Drug ads: $5.2 billion annually—and rising," MoneyWatch, March 11, 2016, https://www.cbsnews.com/news/drug -ads-5-2-billion-annually-and-rising/.

45 Bertha Coombs, "As Obamacare twists in political winds, top insurers made $6 billion (not that there is anything wrong with that)," CNBC Healthcare, August 5, 2017, https://www.cnbc.com/2017/08/05/top -health-insurers-profit-surge-29-percent-to-6-billion-dollars.html.

46 Igor Volsky, 78 Percent of Bankruptcy Filers Burdened by Healthcare Expenses Had Health Insurance, ThinkProgress, June 4, 2009, https ://thinkprogress.org/78-percent-of-bankruptcy-filers-burdened-by -healthcare-expenses-had-health-insurance-c578a0ac38d4/.

47 Abigail Hess, "Here's how much the average student loan borrower owes when they graduate," CNBC Make It, February 15, 2018, https://www.cnbc.com/2018/02/15/heres-how-much-the-average -student-loan-borrower-owes-when-they-graduate.html.

48 Drew DeSilver, "For most U.S. workers, real wages have barely budged in decades." Pew Research Center, Fact Tank: News in the Numbers, October 9, 2014, http://www.pewresearch.org/fact-tank/2014/10/09 /for-most-workers-real-wages-have-barely-budged-for-decades/.

49 "Income Inequality in the United States," Inequality.org, https://in -equality.org/facts/income-inequality/.

50 Robert Frank, "It's true, the rich do get richer—here's why . . .", CNBC, Inside Wealth, November 18, 2014, https://www.cnbc .com/2014/11/18/heres-why-the-rich-do-get-richer.html.

51 Stacy Curtin, "2008 Financial Crisis Cost Americans $12.8 Trillion: Report," YAHOO Finance, September 17, 2012, https://finance.yahoo

.com/blogs/daily-ticker/2008-financial-crisis-cost-americans-12-8-tril
-lion-l45432501.html.

52   David Goldman, "Worst year for jobs since '45," CNN Money,
      January 9, 2009, http://money.cnn.com/2009/01/09/news/economy
      /jobs_december/.

53   Tami Luhby, "Almost half of US families can't afford basics like
      rent and food," CNN Money, May 17, 2018, http://money.cnn
      .com/2018/05/17/news/economy/us-middle-class-basics-study/index
      .html.

54   Peter Janney, *Mary's Mosaic: The CIA Conspiracy to Murder John F.
      Kennedy, Mary Pinchot Meyer, and Their Vision for World Peace* (New
      York: Skyhorse Publishing, 2012), 391.

55   Timothy O'Leary, *Flashbacks: A Personal and Cultural History of an Era*
      (Los Angeles: J.P. Tarcher, Inc.), 190.

56   C. David Heymann, *Georgetown Ladies Social Club: Power, Passion, and
      Politics in the Nation's Capital* (New York: Atria), 203, 168.

57   Nina Burleigh, *A Very Private Woman: The Life and Unsolved Murder of
      Presidential Mistress Mary Meyer* (New York: Bantam, 1998), 259.

58   Richard Belzer and David Wayne, *Hit List: An In-Depth Investigation
      Into The Mysterious Deaths of Witnesses to the JFK Assassination* (New
      York: Skyhorse Publishing, 2016), 79.

59   H. R. Haldeman with Joseph DiMona, *The Ends of Power* (New York:
      Dell, 1978), 39.

60   Tufts University, *Global Development and Environment Institute,
      Macroeconomics in Context,* Goodwin, et al, 2006, Chapter 8, 20.

61   Apple Website, "Identify Counterfeit or Uncertified Lightning
      Connector Accessories."

62   Eric Nellis, *The Long Road to Change: America's Revolution 1750–1820*
      (Peterborough, Canada: Broadview Press, 2007), 249.

63   Hixson, William F., *Triumph of the Bankers: Money and Banking in
      the Eighteenth and Nineteenth Centuries* (London, UK: Praeger, 1993),
      14–15.

64   Peter Knight, *Conspiracy Theories in American History: An Encyclopedia*
      (Santa Barbara, CA: ABC-CLIO, 2003), 362.

65   John L. O'Sulivan, "Annexation, " *United States Magazine and
      Democratic Review,* New York, July-August 1845, Volume 17.

66   "United States Presidents' Inaugural Speeches from Washington to
      George W. Bush," *Project Gutenberg,* August 7, 2008, http://www
      .gutenberg.org/files/925/925-h/925-h.htm#link2H_4_0015.

67   Donald W. Miller Jr., "A Jeffersonian View of the Civil War," LewRockwell.com, September 7, 2001, https://www.lewrockwell.com /2001/09/donald-w-miller-jr-md/a-jeffersonian-view-of-the-civil-war/.

68   Miller.

69   Editorial Section, *The New York Evening Post,* March 12, 1861.

70   Leonard M. Scruggs, "The Morrill Tariff: Northern Provocation to Southern Secession," TarheelTeaParty.org, July 1, 2015, https ://tarheelteaparty.org/?p=16449.

71   Mike Hewitt, "America's Forgotten War Against the Central Banks," *DollarDaze,* October 19, 2007, http://news.goldseek.com /GoldSeek/1192819378.php.

72   Hewitt.

73   Ibid.

74   President Pro Tempore, United States Senate, https://www.senate. gov/ artandhistory/history/common/briefing/President_Pro_Tempore .htm.

75   Mark Hageman, "Lafayette Baker, Union Spymaster (Self Proclaimed Chief of U.S. Intelligence) During American Civil War," Signal Corp Association, (http://www.civilwarsignals.org/pages/spy/lafayettebaker .html).

76   Hageman.

77   John Rhodehamel and Louise Taper, eds., *Right or Wrong, God Judge Me: The Writings of John Wilkes Booth* (Chicago: University of Illinois, 1997), 106.

78   Rhodehamel and Taper, 108.

79   Ibid, 106.

80   Ibid, 116.

81   John K. Lattimer, *Lincoln and Kennedy: Medical & Ballistic Comparisons of Their Assassinations* (New York: Harcourt Brace Jovanovich, 1980), 59.

82   James O. Hall and Michael Maione, *To Make a Fortune—John Wilkes Booth: Following the Money Trail,* 17–18.

83   Ben Pittman, *The Assassination of President Lincoln and the Trial of the Conspirators* (New York: Moore, Wilstach, and Baldwin, 1865), 45.

84   Leonard F. Guttridge and Ray A. Neff, *Dark Union: The Secret Web of Profiteers, Politicians, and Booth Conspirators That Led to Lincoln's Death* (Hoboken, NJ: John Wiley & Sons, 2003), 9–13.

85   Bill O'Reilly and Martin Dugard, *Killing Lincoln: The Shocking Assassination That Changed America Forever* (New York: Henry Holt & Company, 2011), p. 289.

86   Walter Lynwood Fleming, *The Sequel of Appomattox: A Chronicle of the Reunion of the States,* Volume 32 (New Haven, CT: Yale University Press, 1919), 124.

87   George Seldes, *Lords of the Press* (New York: Julian Messner, Inc., 1938), 239.

88   David b. Sachsman and David W. Bulla, editors, *Sensationalism: Murder, Mayhem, Mudslinging, Scandals, and Disasters in 19th-Century Reporting* (New Jersey: Transaction Publishers, 2013), p. 10.

89   Front page, New York *World,* February 17, 1898.

90   John Baker, "Effects of the Press on Spanish-American Relations in 1898," Humboldt State University, October 14, 2007, https://morganparkcps .enschool.org/ourpages/auto/2013/4/4/52667817/The%20Press%20 and%20Spanish-American%20Relations%20in%201898.pdf

91   Platt Amendment, 1903.

92   President William McKinley's War Message to Congress asking for a Declaration of War, April 11, 1898.

93   "The World of 1898: The Spanish-American War," Hispanic Division of the Library of Congress, http://www.loc.gov/rr/hispanic/1898 /chroncuba.html.

94   "Timetable History of Cuba: Struggle for Independence," HistoryofCuba .com, http://www.historyofcuba.com/history/time/timetbl2d.html.

95   *United States, A Treaty of Peace Between the United States and Spain: Message from the President of the United States, Transmitting a Treaty of Peace Between the United States and Spain, Signed at the city of Paris, on December 10, 1898,* [With accompanying papers and map] (Volume 2), (University of Michigan Library, 1899), 564.

96   Alfred Thayer Mann, *The Atlantic Monthly,* December 1, 1890.

97   "Andrew Jackson, Farewell Address, March 4, 1827," The American Presidency Project, http://www.presidency.ucsb.edu/ws/index.php?pid =67087.

98   "Forecast of the gross federal debt of the United States for fiscal years 2017 to 2028," The Statistics Portal, https://www.statista.com /statistics/216998/forecast-of-the-federal-debt-of-the-united-states/.

99   "Interest Expense on the Debt Outstanding," Treasury Direct, https ://www.treasurydirect.gov/govt/reports/ir/ir_expense.html.

100 Dorothy M. Nichols, *Modern Money Mechanics: A Workbook on Bank Reserves and Deposit Expansion* (Federal Reserve Bank of Chicago, 1982), 6.

101 Ellen Brown, "Thinking Outside the Box: How a Bankrupt Germany Solved its Infrastructure Problems," *The Web of Debt,* August 9, 2017, http://www.webofdebt.com/articles/bankrupt-germany.php.

102 Smedley D. Butler, *War is a Racket* (Round Table Press, 1935.)

103 "Dominican Republic Occupation (1916–24)," globalsecurity.org, https://www.globalsecurity.org/military/ops/dominican-republic-1916 .htm.

104 Sidney Lens, *The Forging of the American Empire: A History of American Imperialism From the Revolution to Vietnam* (New York: Thomas Y. Crowell Company, 1974), 214.

105 Lens, 223.

106 "Over Here: World War I on the Home Front," Digital History using new technologies to enhance teaching and research, ID 3478, http ://www.digitalhistory.uh.edu/disp_textbook.cfm?smtid=2&psid=3478.

107 *St. Louis Globe-Democrat,* April 5, 1918.

108 "Treaty of Peace With Germany (Treaty of Versailles)," https://www .loc.gov/law/help/us-treaties/bevans/m-ust000002-0043.pdf.

109 Ike Jeanes, *Forecast and Solution: Grappling With the Nuclear* (Pocahontas Press, 1996), 569.

110 Herbert Hoover, *The Ordeal of Woodrow Wilson* (McGraw-Hill, 1958), 241–42.

111 Charles Lutton, "Pearl Harbor: Fifty Years of Controversy," Institute of Historical Review, Reprinted from *The Journal of Historical Review,* Winter 1991-1992 vol. 11, no. 4, 431–467 (http://ihr.org/jhr/v11 /v11p431_Lutton.html).

112 George Morgenstern, *Pearl Harbor: The Story of the Secret War* (Devin-Adair, 1947), 13–14.

113 Walter Millis, *This is Pearl!: The United States and Japan—1941* (Greenwood Press, 1971), 33–34.

114 Charles Austin Beard, *President Roosevelt and the Coming of War, 1941: A Study in Appearances and Reality* (New Haven: Yale University Press, 1948), 424.

115 Robert Theobald, *The Final Secret of Pearl Harbor* (Devon-Adair Publishers, 1977), 198–200.

116 Robert S. Norris and Hans M. Kristensen, "Global nuclear weapons inventories, 1945–2010," *Bulletin of the Atomic Scientists,* 66:4, 2010, 77–83, DOI: 10.2968/066004008.

117 Gordon H. Chang, "JFK, China, and the Bomb," *Journal of American History,* Vol. 74 No. 4, March 1988, (http://www.jstor.org /pss/1894411).

118 "Vietnam Casualties—The Entire Vietnam War Casualty Profiles," The Vietnam War, December 10, 2012, https://thevietnamwar.info /vietnam-war-casualties/.

119 Sean Kimmons, "For Vietnam, leftover American bombs mean the war has never ended," PRI Public Radio International, May 26, 2014, https://www.pri.org/stories/2014-05-26/vietnam-leftover-american-bombs-mean-war-has-never-ended.

120 William A. Buckingham, Jr., *Operation Ranch Hand: The Air Force and Herbicides in Southeast Asia 1961–1971* (Washington, DC: Office of Air Force History, United States Air Force,1982), Foreword iii-iv.

121 "What is Agent Orange?," The Aspen Institute, https://www.aspeninstitute.org/programs/agent-orange-in-vietnam-program/ what-is-agent-orange/.

122 "Napalm in Vietnam War Development and Early Use," The Vietnam War, January 18, 2014, https://thevietnamwar.info/napalm-vietnam-war/.

123 Erin McGoff, "How the U.S. Secret War in Laos is Still Happening Today," Pulitzer Center, October 27, 2017, https://pulitzercenter.org/reporting/how-us-secret-war-laos-still-happening-today.

124 *Time* Magazine, "From Containment to Isolation," February 18, 1966.

125 George F. Kennan, "Containment: 40 Years Later: Containment Then and Now," *Foreign Affairs*, Spring 1987, https://www.foreignaffairs.com/articles/1987-03-01/containment-40-years-later.

126 Virginia State Board of Education vs. Barnette, Cornell University Law School, Legal Information Institute, June 14, 1943 (http://www.law.cornell.edu/supct/html/historics/USSC_CR_0319_0624_ZC.html).

127 Congressional Record, House, February 12, 1954, 1700.

128 President Eisenhower's Partial Statement Approving House Resolution 243 to Include the Words "Under God" in the Pledge to the Flag, June 14,1954.

129 Lynn, Kenneth O. under the name "Ken Lynn," "The Origin and Meaning of the Pledge of Allegiance," *Freethought Today*, a publication of *The Freedom From Religion* Foundation, May 1999, 7. https://ffrf.org/about/getting-acquainted/item/18510-the-origin-and-meaning-of-the-pledge-of-allegiance.

130 Joint Chiefs of Staff Operation Northwoods Documents.

131 Ibid.

132 John F. Kennedy Presidential Library and Museum website, transcript of Commencement address at American University, June 10, 1963, https://www.jfklibrary.org/Asset-Viewer/BWC7I4C9QUmLG9J6I8oy8w.aspx.

133 James K. Galbraith, "Exit Strategy," *Boston Review*, October/November 2003, http://bostonreview.net/archives/BR28.5/galbraith.html.

134 "Famous Crimes: Lisa Howard," Spartacus Educational, http://sparta
     -cus-educational.com/JFKhowardL2.html.

135 Jonathan Vankin, *The 80 Greatest Conspiracies of all Time* (Citadel,
     2004), 19.

136 "John F. Kennedy: Address in Miami Before the Inter-American Press
     Association," The American Presidency Project, November 18, 1963,
     http://www.presidency.ucsb.edu/ws/?pid=9529.

137 Rich Haney, *Celia Sanchez: The Legend of Cuba's Revolutionary Heart*
     (Algora, New York, 2005), 170.

138 James K. Galbraith, "Exit Strategy," *Boston Review,* October/November
     2003, http://bostonreview.net/archives/BR28.5/galbraith.html.

139 William Manchester, *One Brief Shining Moment: Remembering Kennedy*
     (Little Brown, 1983), 175.

140 Bryan Bender and Neil Swidey, "Robert F. Kennedy saw conspiracy in
     JFK's assassination," *Boston Globe,* November 24, 2013, https://www3
     .bostonglobe.com/metro/2013/11/24/his-brother-keeper-robert-kennedy
     -saw-conspiracy-jfk-assassination/TmZ0nfKsB34p69LWUBgsEJ/story
     .html?arc404=true.

141 William Conrad Gibbons, *The U.S. Government and the Vietnam War:
     Executive and Legislative Roles and Relationships Part III January-July
     1965* (Princeton University Press, 1989), 1–2.

142 Janney, 390–391.

143 Robert F. Kennedy, Jr., "John F Kennedy's Vision of Peace," *Rolling
     Stone*, November 20, 2013, https://www.rollingstone.com/politics
     /news/john-f-kennedys-vision-of-peace-20131120.

144 Leonard Steinhorn, "War, Liberalism, Trust in Government: The
     Many Casualties of LBJ's Gulf of Tonkin Resolution," *The Blog*,
     August 4, 2014, http://www.huffingtonpost.com/leonard-steinhorn
     /why-liberalism-didnt-surv_b_5646136.html.

145 David J. Garrow, *The FBI and Martin Luther King, Jr: From "Solo" to
     Memphis* (W. W. Norton & Co., 1981), 78.

146 "Findings on MLK Assassination," JFK Assassination Records, National
     Archives, https://www.archives.gov/research/jfk/select-committee-report
     /part-2e.html.

147 Excerpt from "The King Conspiracy Exposed in Memphis," James W.
     Douglass; in The Assassinations, edited by James DiEugenio and Lisa
     Pease, 2003, Copyright 2003 by James W. Douglass.

148 "Robert F. Kennedy Autopsy Report," Autopsyfiles.org, http://www
     .autopsyfiles.org/reports/Other/kennedy,%20robert_report.pdf.

149 "Report on the Medicolegal Investigation of Senator Robert F. Kennedy," Mary Ferrell Foundation, https://www.maryferrell.org/showDoc.html?docId=31989#relPageId=1&tab=page.

150 Paul Schrade, Testimony before Sirhan B. Sirhan's Parole Hearing, February 2016.

151 Michael Martinez and Brad Johnson, "Attorneys for RFK convicted killer Sirhan push 'second gunman' argument," CNN, March 12, 2012, https://www.cnn.com/2012/03/04/justice/california-rfk-second-gun/index.html.

152 Bernard K. Duffy and Richard W. Leeman, Editors, *American Voices: An Encyclopedia of Contemporary Orators* (Greenwood, Connecticut, 2005), 244.

153 Bryan Bender and Neil Swidey, "Robert F. Kennedy saw conspiracy in JFK's assassination," *The Boston Globe*, November 24, 2013, https://www3.bostonglobe.com/metro/2013/11/24/his-brother-keeper-robert-kennedy-saw-conspiracy-jfk-assassination/TmZ0nfKsB34p69LWUBgsEJ/story.html?arc404=true.

154 Bill Bonner, "Foolish to Give Up on Gold Now," *Forbes Investing*, January 3, 2012, https://www.forbes.com/sites/greatspeculations/2012/01/03/foolish-to-give-up-on-gold-now/#598e1a975821.

155 Robin Wigglesworth in London, "$6.3 Trillion Wiped Off Global Markets in 2011," CNBC Asia Pacific News, December 30, 2011, https://www.cnbc.com/id/45831478.

156 Richard A. Oppel Jr. and Don Van Natta Jr, "ENRON'S COLLAPSE: THE RELATIONSHIPS; Bush and Democrats Disputing Ties to Enron," *The New York Times*, January 12, 2002, https://www.nytimes.com/2002/01/12/business/enron-s-collapse-the-relationships-bush-and-democrats-disputing-ties-to-enron.html.

157 Ron Callari/Albion Monitor, "The Enron, Cheney, Taliban Connection," *AlterNet*, February 22, 2002, https://www.alternet.org/story/12525/the_enron-cheney-taliban_connection.

158 Hamid Wahed Alikuza, *A Concise History of Afghanistan in 25 Volumes: Volume 14* (Trafford Publishing, 2013), 672.

159 Alikuza, 673.

160 Human Rights Watch, "Enron: History of Human Rights Abuse in India," January 23, 2002, https://www.hrw.org/news/2002/01/23/enron-history-human-rights-abuse-india.

161 Ron Callari and Albion Monitor, "EnronGate: The Enron-Cheney-Taliban Connection," *AlterNet*, February 27, 2002.

162 Michael C. Ruppert, *Crossing the Rubicon: The Decline of the American Empire at the End of the Age of Oil* (New Society Publishers, 2004), 99.